A Brief History of
Vaishnava Saint Poets

THE ALWARS

A Brief History of
Vaishnava Saint Poets

THE ALWARS

Dr. P. Jayaraman

Vani Book Company

Vani Book Company

Head Office

4695, 21-A, Daryaganj, New Delhi 110 002, India
Phone +91 11 23273167 **Fax** : +91 11 23275710

Registered Bookstores and Offices

Ashok Rajpath, Patna 800 004, Bihar
Coffee House Campus, Mahatma Gandhi Marg, Allahabad 211 001, Uttar Pradesh
Mahatma Gandhi International Hindi University, Wardha 442 001, Maharashtra
Sultania Road, Motia Park, Bhopal 462 001, Madhya Pradesh
Goripur Taliya Para, 313, R.B.C. Road 24- Parganas (North) Kolkata 743 166, West Bengal

www.vaniprakashan.in
marketing@vaniprakashan.in
sales@vaniprakashan.in

A Brief History of Vaishnava Saint Poets : THE ALWARS
by Dr. P. Jayaraman

ISBN : 978-93-89012-69-9
Philosophy/Culture/History/Poetry

First Edition 2019
Price : ₹ $ 25.00/£15.00/₹699

Printed & Bound in City Press, Delhi 110 095
Vani Prakashan's signature motif is created by Artist Maqbool Fida Husain

Contents

Preface

The period of Bhakti literature in the Tamil is reckoned by scholars and historians to be between the 5th and the 9th centuries A.D. During this period two major schools of Bhakti philosophy- Saivism and Vaishnavism- were prevalent in the Tamil speaking region of southern India.

To understand Tamil Bhakti literature, an understanding of the basic doctrines of Saivism and Vaishnavism is necessary.

These two major schools of the Bhakti movement developed around Lord Shiva (Saivism) and Lord Vishnu (Vaishnavism) respectively. Through their melodious poems several saintly poets inspired this movement. Saivism was inspired by the distinguished poets Tirumoolar, Appar, Tiru Gyana Sambandar, Tiru Naavukkarasar, Sundara Murti Naayanaar and Manikka Vaachakar. These saintly poets were called Naayanmars who were sixty-three in number.

Vaishnavism was developed and popularized by the saintly poets known as 'Alwars'. There were twelve Alwars and the total number of poems composed by them was 3892. All these poems were compiled and consolidated in the 9th century by Acharya Nathamuni with the help of his preceptor Nammalwar. Later, scholars of Vaishnavism added to this compilation 108 poems presented under the title of Iramanuja Nootrantadi, which had been composed by the Vaishnava Saint and Acharya Ramanuja's honored disciple Tiruvarangattu Amuthanar. Thus, the 12 Alwars' 3892 verses and Amuthanar's 108 verses collectively totaled 4000 verses becoming the 'Tamil Veda' with the title of "Naalaayira Divya Prabandham" [4000 Divine verses]. A complete translation in Hindi (Eleven Volumes) of "Naalaayira Divya Prabandham" preceded this attempt to summarize in English for the benefit of worldwide English readers.

A Brief History of Vaishnava Saint Poets : The Alwars presents an introduction to Naalaayira Divya Prabandham, 12 Alwar saints, their lives, works and philosophy under 8 Chapters; Also, Vaishnava Saint, and Acharya Sri Ramanuja's Disciple Tiruvarangattu Amuthanar and his work Iramanuja Nootrantadi are introduced under Appendix One. Under Appendix Two, an introduction to Vaishnava Saint poets Alwars and Vaishnava philosophers and thinkers called Acharyas is presented.

The works of Alwars are of great importance as they provided the basic philosophical and religious doctrines of Vaishnavism culminating in the school of philosophy- Visishtadvaita, developed by Acharya Ramanuja.

Alwars' names in Tamil and Sanskrit

Tamil names of twelve Alwars are well known. Also, all of them have names in Sanskrit too. Those names are given below. Of course, both Tamil and Sanskrit names of a few Alwars such as Periyalwar, Nammalwar and Tondaradippodi Alwar are used frequently.

In Tamil	In Sanskrit
Poigai Alwar	Saroyogi
Bhootattalwar	Bhootayogi
Peyalwar	Mahayogi
Thirumazhisai Alwar	Bhaktisaara
Kulasekara Alwar	Kulasekara
Periyalwar	Vishnuchitta
Andal	Godha
Nammalvar	Shatagopa
Madhura Kavi Alwar	Madhura kavi
Tondaradippodi Alwar Narayana	Bhaktanghri Renu and Vipra
Tiruppan Alwar	Yogivaaha
Tirumangai Alwar	Parakala

The entire 'Naalaayira Divya Prabandham' was brought out in Hindi under the title of *Sant Vani* (Volumes 1-11) by Shri Arun Maheshwari, Chairman-Vani Prakashan, New Delhi. Mr. Maheshwari had an inherent appreciation for bringing a body of work heretofore known only in the Tamil speaking world to a larger audience. He undertook the publication in Hindi and encouraged the cultivation of an even larger audience by suggesting that at least the notion of the Alwar's work be made available to an English-speaking and reading audience as well. In so doing, the publisher has created a cultural bridge between India and the larger World.

Poigai Alwar
Bhootattalwar
Peyalwar
Tirumazhisai Alwar
Periyalwar
Andal
Kulasekara Alwar
Nammalwar
Madhura Kavi Alwar
Tondadippodi Alwar
Tiruppan Alwar
Tirumanga Alwar

“ओम् नमो नारायणाय”

॥ ஓம் நமோ நாராயணாய ॥

"*OM NAMO NARAYANAYA*"

Acknowledgments

Our heart-felt profound thanks are due to Revered Acharya Arumuganathaswami, Managing Editor, *Hinduism Today* published by Kauai's Hindu Monastery/Himalayan Academy for his kind permission to use in this book, the pictures of 12 Alwars (individual and collective) published in the magazine *Hinduism Today* (January/Febuary/March 2019 issue; pages 40 & 41); in this connection, we are also extremely grateful to Banni Sekhon, the artist of the picture and paramacharya Sadasivanathaswami and Acharya Kumarnathaswami and the esteemed magazine *Hinduism Today*.

I constantly received selfless moral support and help in every possible way and abundant encouragement for years from the following friends and well-wishers which allowed me to work on my books without interruption: Mr. Vijay Kewalramani, Mr. Lal Sani, Mr. Parag Saxena, Mr. Haresh Ramchandani (New York), Dr. Gopal Basisht (Orlando, FL) and Dr. Ravi Prakash Singh (Nashville, TN). I profoundly thank them all.

I offer my heartfelt gratitude to HSR Apparels Inc. and its President Haresh Ramchandani as well as Meg McKernan and Racquel Campbell for their immense support and help in creating an atmosphere in which I could work independently and continually since 2008.

I am greatly indebted to Ms. Esther T. Loewengart (Kalpana) for her brilliant editorial assistance. The entire Book was read and corrected wherever needed by her. I sincerely thank her for patiently spending hours of her time in editing and offering suggestions for making the subject interesting from the readers' point of view and preserving essence of the scripture. Without her dedicated and devoted help, this work could not have come out successfully.

Also, I especially wish to thank Dr. Jim G. Kahn who, without a moment's hesitation, took time from his own considerable work to copy edit the entire manuscript.

I offer my sincere thanks to Mr. Deepak H. Dave, Executive Director, Bharatiya Vidya Bhavan, USA for hours of his technical assistance in computerizing this manuscript. I profusely and profoundly express my sincere thanks to Mr. Deepak H. Dave for all his efforts, editorial assistance and splendid use of his valuable time; I therefore would like to consider him as opulent and superb Editor.

I profusely offer my thanks to the scholarly publisher Shri Arun Maheshwari, Chairman- Vani Prakashan, New Delhi and all dedicated staff members of Vani Prakashan for bringing out this publication in a record time.

With these words, I am pleased to present this Book to the readers who wish to become familiar with the 'Naalaayira Divya Prabandham'. I hope, they will find the study of this book highly rewarding.

Dr. P. Jayaraman
New York
June, 2019

''ओम् नमो नारायणाय''

|| ஓம் நமோ நாராயணாய ||

"OM NAMO NARAYANAYA"

"ओम् नमो नारायणाय"

॥ ஓம் நமோ நாராயணாய ॥

"*OM NAMO NARAYANAYA*"

One

Introduction

A Brief History of the Development of Vaishnavism (also known as Vaishnava Dharma, Vishnu or Narayana worship) in the Tamil speaking region of southern India

Tamil language is one of the oldest among Indian languages. Its literature too is quite ancient. The Tamil literature enjoyed its highest position during the period from 500 B.C. to 200 A. D., during which an association of prominent scholars, called 'Sangam' existed in the well-known city of Madurai. This Sangam served to convene meetings of renowned scholars, poets and learned people. They were the arbiters of the quality, grandeur, scholarship and literary greatness. Only after the Sangam's literary scrutiny could the work move into the ranks of best literature. The Sangam and its association of scholars was patronized by the then ruling Pandiya Kings. Even with royal patronage these Sangams acted autonomously with respect to their literary reviews and decisions. It is believed that these Sangams were three in number, First Tamil Sangam, Middle or Second Tamil Sangam and Last or Third Tamil Sangam which functioned out of Madurai, Kapatapuram and Madurai again respectively. They were supported by Pandiya, Chola & Chera kings as well as smaller rulers and patrons.

Some of the eminent and glorious works such as Tolkappiyam (The oldest and still in use Tamil Grammar), literary works such as Puranaanooru, Ahanaanooru, Patthuppaattu, Paripaadal, Kalittohai, etc. belong to these Sangam periods as well. A few major literary works, such as Chilappadhikaram, and Manimekalai belong to the post- Sangam period 200 A.D. A deep study of the above literary works, especially, Paripaadal, and Chilappadhikaram indicate that even during pre-christen era, Vaishnava Dharma (Vaishnavism) prevailed extensively in the social life of Tamil speaking people. Devotion to Lord Vishnu (Lord Narayana), His ten incarnations and the mythological stories associated with Lord Vishnu had started spreading among the Tamil speaking people. This devotion led to the construction of temples for Lord Vishnu in various places.

Owing to its acceptance by the common people and royal patronage, Vaishnavism had developed extensively in the Tamil speaking region, where Lord Vishnu is called Maal or Tirumaal. A detailed description of Tirumaal (Lord Vishnu), His qualities and Incarnations, is depicted in Paripaadal and Chilappadhikaram. Tirumaal, was accepted as Para-Brahman or Supreme Being, responsible for the universe's creation, sustenance and dissolution (Srishti, Stithi and Laya). Tirumaal is seen as the essence of the Trinity - Brahma, Vishnu and Shiva, and an integrated form of all five elements – earth, water, fire, air and ether. This can be seen in Paripaadal 1- 41-50; 3-61-70. Six long verses are devoted to Tirumaal where 'Para', 'Vyuha', 'Vibhava', 'Antaryami' and 'Archa' forms (a brief explanation of these 5 forms of Tirumaal or Narayana follows) of Lord Vishnu with all His characteristics, qualities and Incarnations are elaborately described.

A few examples-

"Naaval Antanar Arumaraip Porule!"

''ओम् नमो नारायणाय''

॥ ஓம் நமோ நாராயணாய ॥

"*OM NAMO NARAYANAYA*"

''ओम् नमो नारायणाय''

|| ஓம் நமோ நாராயணாய ||

"OM NAMO NARAYANAYA"

'O! embodiment of the Fundamental Principle of all four Vedas, chanted by scholarly Brahmins! Paripaadal 1- 13).'

An ecstatic description of Lord Tirumaal is given in the following poem (Paripaadal 3-63-72).

"Thou art the heat in fire;
The sweet fragrance in a flower;
Thou art the ruby among all precious stones;
Thou art the elegance in eloquent speech;
Thou art love in character;
Thou art the Vedic Hymn;
Thou art the first element Ether among five elements - earth, water, fire, wind and ether.
Thou art the hot rays of sun and the cool rays of the moon; all visible things and their inward qualities art you;
Thou art everything;
Thou art neither created nor the creator, though Thou art responsible for the creation, sustenance and dissolution of the universe."

Paripaadal's Sections 1, 2, 3, 4, 13 and 15 describe the five different forms of Tirumaal (Lord Narayana):

(a) *Para* : Lord Narayana dwelling with his consort Sridevi in Vaikunta - transcendental abode.

(b) *Vyuha* : Lord Narayana in yogic slumber, lying on Adisesha bed in the milky ocean being worshipped by Devas (celestial beings).

(c) *Vibhava* : Lord Narayana manifesting in different Incarnations for the protection of dharma.

(d) *Antaryami* : The In- dweller and all-pervasive form in all beings.

(e) *Archa* : The Divine incarnation in idols and images, worshipped by people in their homes and temples.

The major post-sangam epic Chilappadhikaram (second century A.D.) presents a very clear example of widespread Vaishnavism in the Tamil speaking region. In particular, we can take the Section "Aaychiyar Kuravai" (Part 2 - Madurai, Section 17, Verse 14). There we see the description of shepherd girls dancing in the background of melodious devotional music, in a village close to Madurai which can be compared to 'Gopika Geetam' appearing in Srimad Bhagavatam.

Chilappadhikaram provides an extensive and artistic description of Vaishnavism, precisely Narayana worship in particular. It is a prayer song addressed to Lord Narayana's Incarnation as Krishna, seeking His protection from evil. The song describes the attributes of Lord Narayana in His Different Incarnations- eg. Vaamana, Rama, Krishna etc. and the divine acts associated with these specific incarnations. The shepherd girls, praising the attributes of Lord Narayana, ask :

What is the use of ears which do not hear the divine qualities of Tirumaal, that is Narayana?
What is the use of eyes which do not see the unique greatness of Lord Narayana?
What is the use of a tongue which does not pronounce the eight-lettered mantra - OM! Namo Narayanaya?

(ॐ नमो नारायणाय)

(Tirumaal seer kelaatha Sevi enna Seviye?
Kariyavanaik kaanaatha Kannenna Kanne?
Naaraayana! Ennaa Naavenna Nave?)

—*Aaychiyar Kuravai, Verse 14*

"ओम् नमो नारायणाय"

|| ஓம் நமோ நாராயணாய ||

"*OM NAMO NARAYANAYA*"

“ओम् नमो नारायणाय”

॥ ஓம் நமோ நாராயணாய ॥

"OM NAMO NARAYANAYA"

In the fifth century A.D., the South India experienced an atmosphere of social tranquility and political stability. This was a time, when Vaishnavism had extensive patronage from the Pandiya and Pallava Kings. With their patronage temples for Lord Vishnu (Narayana) were constructed in many cities. In Perur, for example, in the 7th and 8th centuries, a Vishnu temple was constructed by Varaguna Pandiyan. In Kanchipuram, during the same period Vaikunta Perumal Temple was built by Pallava Ruler Nandi Varman, II. Other temples were constructed in different areas with the patronage of the then rulers.

As a result of this royal patronage, and also through the Alwar saints and their devotional, spiritual and philosophic poems, Vaishnavism thrived from the 5th century to 9th century A.D. throughout the southern part of India.

Vaishnava Alwar Saint Poets & their History

Between the 5th and 9th centuries A.D., there were twelve Vaishnava Devotional Saint Poets, called Alwars (also written as Azhwars), who had composed 3,892 verses in ancient Tamil language. These verses were collected and edited by the first Vaishnava Acharya Nathamuni, during the 9th and 10th Centuries A.D. Nathamuni had been inspired and taught by Nammalwar, also known as Shatagopa, the propounder of Tamil Veda.

Alwar means the one “immersed” or “the one who remains enchanted”. In the context of Tamil Alwars, the Appellation refers to the saint poets who remained immersed in devotion to Lord Vishnu or Narayana. These Alwars were twelve in number; and their names are Poigai Alwar, Bhootattalwar, Peyalwar, Tirumazhisai Alwar, Kulasekara Alwar, Periyalwar, Andal, Nammalwar, Madhura Kavi Alwar, Tondaradippodi Alwar, Tiruppanalwar and Tirumangai Alwar.

The number of verses composed by these Alwars was 3892. Tiruvarangattu Amuthanar's work Iramanuja Nootrantadi (in eulogy of Amuthanar's Guru Acharya Ramanuja, the Founder of Visishtadvaita School of Philosophy, 12th century A.D.) consiststing of 108 verses was added as the last treatise to the Alwars' divine verses due to the honor given to his disciple by Acharya Ramanuja. Therefore, the sacred Book of Alwars became well-known as Naalaayira Divya Prabandham, meaning 4000 Divine Verses.

[Naalayira means 4000 in Tamil; 3892 + 108]

The Alwars' verses describe their individual experience of devotion to Lord Narayana. Beyond their personal experience of Narayana, the Alwars composed verses, on the emancipatory principle of devotion to Lord Narayana, affording all human beings irrespective of color, caste and gender, a path to be freed from sin.

This path of devotion to Lord Narayana became extremely popular, according public acceptance of Vaishnavism. The Alwars themselves were the proofs of this liberal attitude. They represented different castes and genders. Nammalwar was from the Vellala caste (Vaishya); Tirumangai Alwar was a Kallar (Shudra); Tiruppanalwar also belonged to (Shudra); Kulasekara Alwar was a king (Kshatriya). While remaining Alwars were Brahmins. Andal, the adopted daughter of Periyalwar was a renowned woman Alwar.

In brief, Divya Prabandham is a treasure of spiritual knowledge and Vaishnava bhakti philosophy and is revered as Veda for its spirituality and sanctity.

''ओम् नमो नारायणाय''

॥ ஓம் நமோ நாராயணாய ॥

"*OM NAMO NARAYANAYA*"

"ओम् नमो नारायणाय"

॥ ஓம் நமோ நாராயணாய ॥

"OM NAMO NARAYANAYA"

For Alwars, Bhakti and Prapatti (Devotion and Self Surrender at the feet of the Lord) are not only the journey but also the destination. For Alwars, the universe is not an illusion to be distanced from, but the multi- faceted expression of their personal, beloved God. Alwars in their verses describe and worship the Lord's existence in the following five forms (Described earlier in the context of Paripaadal):

Para, Vyuha, Vibhava, Antaryami and Archavatara

1. *Para* : Lord Narayana with His consort Sri Devi dwelling in His Transcendental abode-Vaikunta being worshipped by eternal divinities;
2. *Vyuha* : Lord Narayana laying on Adisesha in yoga nidra in the Milky Ocean;
3. *Vibhava* : Lord Narayana in different incarnations / Avataras - Rama, Krishna and eight more Avataras - Lord's descent to the earth for the purpose of protecting dharma;
4. *Antaryami* : Lord as all-pervading spirit, dwelling within all His creations;
5. *Archa* : Divine Incarnation in the consecrated idols and images, worshipped by the devotees, in temples, shrines and homes.

There is no extant authentic historical material regarding the lives of the Alwars. As a result, we depend on descriptions narrated by the Alwars themselves in "Naalaayira Divya Prabandham", as well as accounts by scholars such as Divya Suri Charitam [by Garuda Vahana Panditar], Guru Parampara Prabhavam [by Perumal Geeyar], Prapanna-Amrutam [by Sri Anantacharya Swamy], etc.

First three Alwar Poets-Poigai Alwar, Bhootattalwar and Peyalwar, their lives, works and philosophic principles expressed through their Antadi verses.

A study of these Alwars' works tells us that these three Alwars were highly learned and had developed expertise in ancient scriptures, such as Vedas, Upanishads and Bhagavad Gita. Their only objective was:

- To promote the worship of Lord Vishnu (Narayana).
- To sing the attributes of Lord Narayana.
- To sing the glory of Bhakti (devotion) & Prapatti (surrender).
- To offer service to Lord Narayana.
- To describe Lord Vishnu's Incarnations, especially of Varaha, Vamana, Rama and Krishna.

All three Alwars were supreme Bhaktas of Lord Narayana and they declared devotion as the best of all courses of Sadhana (methods of meditative practice).

These three Alwars were born in the 5th - 6th centuries.

Poigai Alwar was born in Kanchipuram, Bhootattalwar in Mahabalipuram and Peyalwar in Mailapur (Tiru Mayilai).

Among all Alwars, the very first was Poigai Alwar who was a contemporary of both Bhootattalwar and Peyalwar. Since they were contemporaries of one another, they were always collectively called "Mudalalwar"(the first Alwars); each of them composed 100 poems in praise of Lord Narayana. They were called First (Mudal Tiruvantadi), Second (Irandam Tiruvantadi), and Third Tiruvantadi (Moonram Tiruvantadi) respectively. Their poems are considered to have been composed in an ecstatic state resulting from

''ओम् नमो नारायणाय''

॥ ஓம் நமோ நாராயணாய ॥

"OM NAMO NARAYANAYA"

‘‘ओम् नमो नारायणाय’’

॥ ஓம் நமோ நாராயணாய ॥

"*OM NAMO NARAYANAYA*"

a divine vision of Lord Narayana that they had at Tirukkovalur. Because they were deeply immersed in devotion to Lord Narayana, and nothing else, nothing is known about their worldly existence. What we have is the legacy of their Philosophic Vision.

Poigai Alwar
Eulogy of Poigai Alwar and his Antadi

The Sri Vaishnava Saint Mudali Aandaan eulogized effulgent and splendid poet Poigai Alwar born in Kanchipuram. He became identified with the place of his birth Poigai (meaning Pond) filled with fragrant screwpine flowers. He composed the first divine Nootrantadi (hundred Antadi poems) in sweet Tamil language for the benefit of Vaishnava devotees and brightened the entire universe with the light of knowledge described below.

Poigai Alwar's Philosophy

How to attain the Lord Narayana? Poigai Alwar's answer to this major question was as follows:

Lord Narayana and His Grace are attainable only through Devotion to Lord Narayana; Be devoted to Him; Achieve His Grace; Attain Devotion by His Grace.

Alwar instructs his mind: "O My Mind! Meditate on Lord Narayana; bow at His feet whose Incarnations protect the universe and destroy demonic power." (Verse 100 of the first Nootranadi).

Poigai Alwar's mind and psyche remained engrossed in devotion to Lord Narayana. Alwar had derived great happiness, thinking about the Lord's Existence in his heart (verse 99). He felt that with the help of his

Poigai Alwar

பொய்கை ஆழ்வார்

ஓரடியும் சாடுதைத்த ஒண்மலர் சேவடியும்
ஈரடியும் காணலாம் எந் எநஞ்சே-- ஓரடியில்
தாயவனைக் கேசவனைத் தண்டுழாய் மாலை சேர்
மாயவனையே மனத்து வை!

(முதல் திருவந்தாதி, பாசுரம்100)

**Oradiyum saadutaitta onmalar sevadiyum
Eeradiyum kaanalaam en nenje -- oradiyil
Taayavanaik kesavanait randuzhaay
maalaiser Mayavanaiye Manattu vai!
[Alwar's First Tiruvantadi; Verse 100]**

**"How to attain Lord Narayana?
Poigai Alwar 's answer is as follows:"
"Meditate on Lord Narayana; With utter devotion,
bow at His feet Whose incarnations
protect the universe and destroy demonic power."
[Alwar's First Tiruvantadi; Verse 100]**

"ओम् नमो नारायणाय"

॥ ஓம் நமோ நாராயணாய ॥

"*OM NAMO NARAYANAYA*"

tongue, he could easily chant the most sacred eight letter mantra "Om Namo Narayanaya" (ॐ नमो नारायणाय). "Then what is the use of chanting His Sahasra Nama (thousand names)! (verse 95). I will never praise any deity other than Tirumal (Lord Narayana). [verse 64]." Alwar not only praised the Lord's attributes and the beauty of His form, but also His Holy shrines- Sri Venkata Mountain, Sri Vaikunta, Tiruvehka and Tirukkovalur. In addition, Alwar also has described his ecstatic experience of the Archa (Image Incarnation) form of Lord Narayana worshipped in those shrines.

Alwar believed that even uttering their names, would eradicate a person's sins and bless him the Lord's grace (verse 77).

Alwar worshipped the holy Place of Srirangam, and Sri Ranganatha the Presiding Deity of that shrine. (verse 6).

According to Alwar, worshipping Lord Narayana by thought, utterance and action constituted his sole duty (verse 88). Lord Narayana is the Supreme Brahman who is the protector of even Lord Shiva. (verse 74)

Bhootattalwar
Eulogy of Bhootattalwar and his Antadi

Sri Vaishnava Saint Tirukkuruhaip Piran Pillan, the disciple of Acharya Ramanuja, eulogized the Second Tiruvantadi composed by the second Alwar– Bhootatattalwar, describing in the first verse of his divine writing, "I lit the lamp of devotion in order to have the sacred vision of Lord Narayana, as well as to offer that vision to all others in the universe." The Saint Pillan also says, "I sing the sacred refuge at the Divine feet of Bhootattalwar that releases me from the cycle of birth and death (Transmigration)." Here Saint Pillan explains the Dasa Bhakti- as Vaishnavism propounds ie. devotion to the Lord Narayana's devotee.

Bhootattalwair
பூதத்தாழ்வார்

நகரிழைத்து நித்திலத்து நாண்மலர் கொண்டு ஆங்கே
திகழுமணி வயிரம் சேர்த்து --- நிகரில்லாப்
பைங்கமல மேந்திப் பணிந்தேன் பனிமலராள்
அங்கம் வலம கொண்டான் அடி.

(இரண்டாம் திருவந்தாதி, பாசுரம் 4)

Naharizhaittu nittilattu naanmalar kondu aange
Tihazhumani Vairam serttu --- nikarillaap
PainKamala menthip Paninthen panimalaraal
Angam valam kondaan adi!
[Alwar's Second Tiruvantadi; Verse 4]

**"Alwar was devoted to Lord Narayana;
he made his heart the Lord's abode,
decorated that abode with beautiful flower petals
and showered flowers with deep devotion
at the divine feet of the Lord."
[Alwar's Second Tiruvantadi; Verse 4]**

‘‘ओम् नमो नारायणाय’’

॥ ஓம் நமோ நாராயணாய ॥

"OM NAMO NARAYANAYA"

Alwar is Narayana’s devotee, Pillan in turn is the devotee of Alwar, thus the lineage of Dasa Bhakti is established.

Bhootattalwar was devoted to Lord Narayana that he made his heart the Lord’s abode, decorated that abode with beautiful flower petals and showered flowers with deep devotion at the divine feet of the Lord. This was the daily routine of Alwar.
(verse 4)

Alwar gave great importance to the chanting of and meditation on, the divine names of the Lord.
(verses 39 & 41)

According to Alwar, chanting the Lord’s various names and describing His beautiful form, attributes and supremacy endowed the chanter with divinity.
(verses 2 & 44)

Alwar guided his own mind as well as that of the common people to go on the path of devotion to Lord Narayana by three methods: mind (through meditation), speech (chanting of names) and action (worshiping the Lord).
(verse 51)

Alwar had the divine vision of the Lord within himself and surrendered his mind and heart at the feet of the Lord Narayana.
(verse 7)

For Alwar, Lord Narayana is Para Brahma, the Supreme Being. He believed and made his mind understand that,

- “The entire universe and all its activities,
- All supporting Five elements Earth, water, fire, air and ether.
- All bodies and all five senses made up of the elements,

- All creations, sustenance and dissolution of nature, and lives- all are Lord Narayana, the Supreme Being, i.e. 'Para Brahma'".

(verse 24)

Further, he said that despite having all these attributes and being all-comprehensive, Lord Narayana descends to the earth in different incarnations, Rama, Krishna, Vamana, Varaha & Kurma, etc. manifesting Himself in Sri Venkata Hill (Tirumalai or Tirupati) and other holy places and shrines, Srirangam etc. with a view to protecting the pious- good people and devotees.
(verses 25, 29, 30)

According to Alwar, "Tozhuvaar Paadam Tozhuvadu Chirappu" [Worshipping the feet of those who worship at the feet of the Lord Narayana is greater than worshipping the Lord Himself*]
(verse 43)

Peyalwar
Eulogy of Peyalwar and his Antadi

Vaishnava Saint Kurukai Kavalappan, the disciple of Acharya Nathamuni, eulogized the Narayana Bhakti and Prapatti of the third Alwar, Peyalwar. Peyalwar had a beautiful vision of Lord Narayana accompanied by His consort Sri Devi at the sacred place of Tirukkovalur where the Alwar took shelter on a rainy day along with Poigai Alwar and Bhootattalwar. The Saint Kavalappan offered prayers at the sacred feet of Peyalwar who composed 100 ecstatic verses beginning with the words "Tiru Kanden" (I had a beautiful vision of Tiru-Lord Narayana and Sri Devi). It was Alwar's desire that the whole universe has this blissful vision of Lord Narayana. Here also, we find Saint Kavalappan's description of Dasa Bhakti.

''ओम् नमो नारायणाय''

|| ஓம் நமோ நாராயணாய ||

"*OM NAMO NARAYANAYA*"

Peyalwair
பேயாழ்வார்

"கவியினார் கை புனைந்து கண்ணார் கழல் போய்
செவியினார் கேள்வியராய் சேர்ந்தார் -- புவியினார்
போற்றியுரைக்கப் பொலியுமே பின்னைக்காய்
எற்றுயிரை அட்டான் எழில் !"
(மூன்றாம் திருவந்தாதி. பாசுரம் 85)

"Kaviyinaar Kai punainthu kannaar Kazhal poy
Seviyinaar kelviyaraay Sernthar -- puviyinaar
Potriuraikkap poliyume Pinnaikkaay
Etruyirai attaan ezhil !"
(Moontraam Tiruvantadi -- Paasuram 85)

"Alwar describes the qualities of Lord Narayana as incomprehensible and inexpressible. He further states that it was impossible even for the entire universe to collectively chant and hear all His attributes.
[Alwar's Third Tiruvantadi, Verse 85]

Peyalwar described the qualities of Lord Narayana as incomprehensible, and inexpressible. He stated that it was impossible even for the entire universe to collectively chant and hear all His attributes or to recount the 'Lila' (Playful acts) performed by Him in his different incarnations.
(verse 85)

Alwar prescribed different paths of unsurpassed devotion (Bhakti) focusing entirely on Lord Narayana and self-surrender oneself at His feet (Prapatti) enabling the devotee to release himself from all sins.
(verse 88)

Alwar expressed his profound happiness at finding Him, having searched for the Lord with the lamp of knowledge and kept Him in his heart, where he had full confidence that he would always remain.
(verse 94)

According to Peyalwar, Lord Narayana resides in the following places:
on Adisesha in the milky ocean;
Holy shrines such as Sri Venkata Hill, Kanchipuram, Tiruvehka, Tiruvelukkai, Tiruvaipadi, Tiiruvallikeni,
as well as in the heart of Alwar.
(verses 16 and 26)

This is a description of Vyuha, and Archa forms of Lord Narayana. Alwar also described the Vibhava form of Lord Narayana; Narayana in His Different Incarnations as Vamana, Kurma, Rama, Krishna, Varaha, etc. and their 'Lilas' for the protection of the universe, dharma, destruction of injustice and adharma.
(verses 5, 46, 52,54 & 58)

''ओम् नमो नारायणाय''

॥ ஓம் நமோ நாராயணாய ॥

"*OM NAMO NARAYANAYA*"

''ओम् नमो नारायणाय''

॥ ஓம் நமோ நாராயணாய ॥

"OM NAMO NARAYANAYA"

First three Alwar Poets, their meeting and prayers to the Lord Narayana

These first three Alwar poets lived away from society and used to go on pilgrimages.

The first three Alwars, in the course of their pilgrimages, met in a village named Tirikkovalur very close to the well-known sacred city of Tiruvannamalai on a stormy night, never having met before.

Poigai Alwar came there first, and to escape the stormy rain, he took shelter in a small enclosure of a house. There, he laid down to sleep.

Shortly thereafter, Bhootattalwar reached same spot and thought of resting there as well until the rain stopped. There he saw Poigai Alwar sleeping and thought that the space was indeed quite small. But, if one person can lay down at a place, two persons can easily sit there. Poigai invited him inside.

After some time, Peyalwar too, happened to come there looking for shelter. He saw the little space and two persons sitting there and thought that if two can sit, then three can easily stand. He joined them in the enclosure. All three Alwars standing inside the small space started talking about Lord Narayana, His attributes and their Devotion to Lord Narayana. Suddenly, they felt the presence of a fourth person(Entity). As it was pitch dark they could not see anything and could not identify, whose presence it was. There was no lamp; and even if there had been one, how would they have lit it?

Ultimately, they realized that it was none other the Lord Narayana with His Consort Sri Devi.

Then Poigai Alwar, Bhootattalwar and Peyalwar started singing in verses praising Lord Narayana, His beautiful form, glory, qualities, and His incarnations as Rama, Krishna, Varaha, and Vamana etc. Each of the Alwars sang a hundred verses in Antadi style (Antadi – A Verse form in which the last word or sound of a verse becomes the first word or sound of the next verse- An ancient version of 'Antakshari')

These verses are called Tiruvantadi (Divine verses composed in Antadi form); the compilation of these Alwars' (Poigai Alwar, Bhootattalwar and Peyalwar) verses is called Muthal Tiruvantadi (First Divine Verses) Irandam Tiruvantadi (Second Divine Verses) and Moonram Tiruvantadi (Third Divine Verses) respectively.

The English translation of the first verse of each Tiruvantadi of these three Alwars is as follows:

1. Poigai Alwar

   Verse starting with "Vaiyam takaliya"

   Translation:
   I make the earth as a lamp, treat the sea water as clarified
   butter and turn the shining sun light as luminous wick
   (with the help of which I can light the lamp).
   With this lighted lamp, I will try to see the stranger
   whose presence we feel but cannot see.

2. Bhootattalwar

   Verse starting with "Anbe Takaliya"

   I make bhakti (devotion) the lamp; keen desire, like clarified butter, and the mind-melting with devotion, as its wick; I have lit the lamp of knowledge to recognize who the stranger is.

3. Peyalwar

   Verse starting with "Tiruk kanden"

   On having the effulgent Vision of Lord Narayana holding luminous conch and discus in His hands and accompanied by Sri Devi, Peyalwar started singing with delight.

"ओम् नमो नारायणाय"

|| ஓம் நமோ நாராயணாய ||

"*OM NAMO NARAYANAYA*"

" குலம் தரும் செல்வம் தந்திடும் அடியார்
படுதுயர் ஆயின எல்லாம்
நிலந்தரம் செய்யும் நீள் விசும்பு அருளும்
அருளொடு பெருநிலம் அளிக்கும்
பலம் தரும் மற்றும் தந்திடும் பெற்ற
தாயினும் ஆயின செய்யும்
நலம் தரும் சொல்லை நான் கண்டுகொண்டேன்
நாராயணா என்னும் நாமம் !"
(பெரிய திருமொழி ; பாசுரம் 1 / 1 / 9)

" Kulam Tarum selvam tanthidum adiyaar
Padutuyar Aayina Ellam
Nilantaram seyyum neel visumbu arulum
Arulodu perunilam alikkum
Balam Tarum matrum tanthidum Petra
Taayinum Aayina seyyum
Nalam Tarum sollai Naan kandu konden
Narayana ennum Naamam ! "
(Periya Tirumozhi ; Verse 1 / 1 / 9)

ALWAR believes:
"The holy name of Narayana
is the harbinger of all great things,
such as power, noble family and wealth,
and eliminates sorrows of the devotee;
I found all good things by
chanting the sacred name of Narayana "
PERIYA TIRUMOZHI 1/1/9

Tirumangai Alwar

திருமங்கை ஆழ்வார்

Two

Tirumazhisai Alwar

Tirumazhisai Alwar, the fourth among the Alwar saints, was born in the fifth-sixth century A.D. at the sacred pilgrimage site of Tirumazhisai, close to today's Kanchipuram; hence he is called Tirumazhisai Alwar by the name of his birth-place. He was also a disciple of the third Alwar – Peyalwar.

It is believed that like the first three Alwars, Tirumazhisai Alwar was a Yogi. All four Alwars met during their journies to Vaishnava shrines.

The place Tirumazhisai was also known by the name "Mahisaara" (the Essence of the earth). Tirumazhisai Alwar who was born at Mahisaara, was called 'Bhakti-Saara' (Embodiment of Devotion) because of his ecstatic devotion to Lord Narayana.

Tirumazhisai Alwar was absorbed in yogic practices from his childhood and studied the then prevalent Bauddha, Jaina, other religious scriptures and various systems of philosophy* in an effort to gain access to the knowledge of Supreme Being. At the outset he was a staunch follower of Shaivism; at that time, he was known by the name Shiva Vaakya. Later he became the disciple of the third Alwar, Peyalwar and under his influence adopted Vaishnavism. He went on pilgrimages to the prominent Vaishnava shrines at Srirangam, Tiruvallikkeni, Tiruvehka, Sri Venkatadri (Tirupati), Tiruvallur

‘‘ओम् नमो नारायणाय’’

|| ஓம் நமோ நாராயணாய ||

"*OM NAMO NARAYANAYA*"

‘‘ओम् नमो नारायणाय’’

॥ ஓம் நமோ நாராயணாய ॥

"*OM NAMO NARAYANAYA*"

and Kumbhakonam. He immersed himself in the devotional practices of those shrines. Meditating on Lord Narayana, he reached a deep state of ecstasy.

Two literary, devotional and philosophic works, Naanmukan Tiruvantadi and Tiruchchanda viruttam containing 96 verses and 120 verses respectively, are attributed to Tirumazhisai Alwar.

The first treatise, ‘Naanmukan Tiruvantadi’, begins with the word “Naanmukan” which means “four- faced Brahma- the Creator”. Hence, the work itself was given the name Naanmukan Tiruvantadi.

It is also called Naankaam Tiruvantadi; that is “the fourth Antadi”. Since it follows the first three Alwar’s Antadi treatises.

The first verse reads as follows:

“Naanmukanai Naarayanan Padaithaan Naanmukanum
Taan mukamaaich Sankaranait taan padaittaan yaan mukamaai
Antadi melittu arivitten aazh porulai
Chintaamal konmin neer ternthu.”

[All-pervading Lord Narayana created four- faced Brahma;
Then Brahma created Sankara (Lord Shiva);
it proves the great principle of Lord Narayana being the Supreme Being;
I, the devotee of Lord Narayana, am explaining this principle to you through this Antadi;
please keep this sacred principle in your heart]

Bhakti-Saara/Tirumazhisai Alwar concludes this treatise with the Upanishadic declaration that Supreme Spirit pervades the entire universe. This supreme spirit is the Para-brahmatwa of Lord Narayana. According to

Alwar, Lord Narayana is all-pervading inner self of all beings– movable and immovable beings as corroborated by the above Upanishadic Statements.

Alwar says in the last verse (96):

"I realized, Lord Shiva and four-faced Brahma and all deities adore and worship Narayana. He is the primordial Lord and primary cause of the entire universe. I also understood that Lord Narayana Himself represents all past, present and future creations."

Having experienced the grace of the divine form, attributes and adored Incarnations of the Supreme Lord Narayana and having been over-awed by His limitless kindness, the supreme devotee Tirumazhisai Alwar spread among man-kind the message of profound devotion to the Supreme Lord. Alwar's prime objective was to establish the predominance of Lord Narayana over the trinity - Brahma, Vishnu and Shiva as well as other deities, and His Omnipresence, All - Pervasiveness - in short, His Para-Brahmatwa. (the quality of being Supreme Spirit).

We can take verse 20 from Naanmukan Tiruvantadi as an example of Alwar's deep conviction and the influence of his preceptor Peyalwar.

Establishing the all-pervasiveness of Lord Narayana, Alwar addresses the Lord,

"O Lord Narayana! You are the creator and controller of the entire universe, You are the Master of all deities and You are the movable and immovable objects, five elements, the mountains, the sun, the moon and all the galaxies of stars in the cosmos; as such, whatever is and is not in the universe (Being and non-being- all) everything is You!"

(verse 20)

The essence of this verse is - Lord Narayana is the Truth of truths; Supreme Being of all beings.

''ओम् नमो नारायणाय''

|| ஓம் நமோ நாராயணாய ||

"*OM NAMO NARAYANAYA*"

"ओम् नमो नारायणाय"

॥ ஓம் நமோ நாராயணாய ॥

"*OM NAMO NARAYANAYA*"

As explained earlier, according to Tirumazhisai Alwar, Lord Narayana created Brahma; and Brahma created Shiva (Rudra). Lord Narayana is the all-pervading, omnipotent and omnipresent Supreme Spirit–Brahman as expressed in the Upanishads. Alwar says, Lord Narayana is the cause for the whole universe; whatever was and is here and whatever will be here; Everything, the past, the Present and the future are only Lord Narayana.

(verses 1 & 96, Nanmukhan Tiruvantadi)

Tirumazhisai Alwar's second treatise is "Tiruch-Chanda-Viruttam" (Divine Poetic literature composed in the melodious meter- 'Chand Viruttam') consisting of 120 verses. Most of these verses eulogize Lord Narayana, describing His Incarnations (Avataras), especially those of Rama, Krishna, Vaamana, Varaha and Narasimha Avataras, their attributes, Leelas (acts), unique qualities and the sacredness of divine Vaishnava shrines (Divya kshetras), such as Srirangam, Kumbhakonam, etc.

As in the previous treatise, here also Alwar's philosophy of deep devotion to Lord Narayana and Prapatti (surrender) at the Lord's feet, omnipresence, all-pervasiveness and fullness of the Lord as Brahman (Supreme Being) are described elaborately.

Additionally, Alwar counseled all human beings to stay away from any deity other than Lord Narayana. Alwar had full faith in the basic doctrine of Vaishnava Dharma (philosophy)- "Anyatha Sharanam Naasti" [there is no refuge for a devotee other than Lord Narayana] and "Rakshishyateeti Vishwasaha" (a devotee has full trust of being protected only at the feet of Narayana).

(Verse 87)

Alwar's sole devotion to Lord Narayana and his supplication for the grace of the Lord find place in many verses in this treatise. Also denoted are Alwar's full faith in the Lord's unbounded affection for the devotees and His extreme power. Alwar's goal of complete communion with the Divine Being through yogic trance is also described in this treatise.

In summary, Tiruchchanda Viruttam presents a compelling description of the uniqueness of all-pervading Lord Narayana as Brahman (Supreme Being), performing all three functions- creation, sustenance and dissolution (Srushti, Stithi and Laya) of the universe and providing emancipation to his devotees and dependents.
(verses 10 & 17)

"ओम् नमो नारायणाय"

॥ ஓம் நமோ நாராயணாய ॥

"*OM NAMO NARAYANAYA*"

Kulasekara Alwar

குலசேகர ஆழ்வார்

"செடியாய வல் வினைகள் தீர்க்கும் திருமாலே!
நெடியானே வெங்கடவா நின் கோயிலின் வாசல்
அடியாரும் வானவரும் அரம்பையரும் கிடந்தியங்கும்
படியாய்க் கிடந்து உன் பவளவாய் காண்பேனே ! "
(பெருமாள் திருமொழி. ; பாசுரம் 4 / 9)

"Sediyaaya val vinaikal teerkkum Tirumaale !
Nediyaane Venkatavaa Nin koyilin vaasal
Adiyaarum vaanavarum arampaiyarum kidanthiyankum
Padiyaayk kidanthu un Pavalavaay kaanpene ! "
(Perumaal Tirumozhi, Verse 4/ 9)

**ALWAR was a dedicated devotee of Lord Narayana,
particularly in His Incarnation as Rama;
hence desired to be in close proximity to Him
and would have cherished
becoming even a stepping stone
at the entrance to His Sanctum Sanctoram,
on which Vaishnava devotees, heavenly devotees and artists etc. walk.
(PERUMAL TIRUMOZHI 4/9)**

Three

Kulasekara Alwar

In eulogy of Kulasekara Alwar, Sri Vaishnava Acharya Sri Ramanuja– founder of the Visishtadwaita School of philosophy– and the well- known Vaishnava Acharya Manakkal Nambi have both said, “Kulasekara Alwar was a great devotee of Lord Narayana (Sri Ranganatha the presiding deity of Srirangam Temple), author of devotional lyrical hymns in praise of Lord Narayana and staunch devotee of Narayana Bhaktas.”

Kulasekara was a King of the Chera dynasty who ruled over the whole of South India. He was also a dedicated devotee of Lord Narayana, particularly in His incarnation as Rama.

Kulasekara Alwar sought to be in close proximity to Lord Tirumal (Narayana; also known by the name Srinivasa- the presiding deity of Tiruvenkatam, a most sacred place).

If it brought him closer to the lord, Alwar would have cherished becoming even a stepping stone at the entrance to His Sanctum Sanktorum (Perumal Tirumozhi 4/9).

Kulasekara Alwar, the Vaishnava saint of the 8th Century A.D. was a ruler of the Chera dynasty. He ruled over the Kerala region in the south.

“ओम् नमो नारायणाय”

|| ஓம் நமோ நாராயணாய ||

"*OM NAMO NARAYANAYA*"

"ओम् नमो नारायणाय"

॥ ஓம் நமோ நாராயணாய ॥

"*OM NAMO NARAYANAYA*"

The internal references available in "Perumal Tirumozhi", a work of Alwar, reveal that his rule also extended to the Chola and Pandya kingdoms. This means that Kulasekara Alwar was the ruler of the entire Southern region. (Tamilnadu and Kerala).

Besides being a ruler Kulasekara was an earnest devotee of Lord Narayana, especially Narayana's incarnation as Rama, known also as Perumal, meaning 'Great Lord'. Because of this, Alwar too, is called Perumal and he became known as 'Kulasekara Perumal'. "Perumal Tirumozhi" written by Kulasekara Alwar explicated Alwar's devotion to Lord Narayana in His incarnations as Rama and Krishna. Although Kulasekara was a ruler, kingdom held no appeal for him. He was immersed in deep devotion to the Lord, and His devotees. Kulasekara was very much interested in listening to the Vedas, treatises (Shastras) and Puranas, especially Ramayana. He was very eager to renounce his kingdom and to go to the holy city of Srirangam, where he could have the company of Vaishnava devotees. He used to invite Vaishnava saints, scholars and devotees to his palace to listen to their discourses and discussions relating to the scriptures and Puranas. His absorption in the stories of Ramayana was so complete that while hearing them he appeared to be experiencing the incidents as if they were happening in front of him.

In this context, some prominent incidents from his lifetime are given below. One, occurred during a discourse on Ramayana. On hearing the speaker narrate the incident in which demon Khara, accompanied by an army of 14,000 demons had attacked Sri Rama, who was all alone.

Deeply Distressed by Lord Rama's urgent need for help, Kulasekara ordered his own army to assemble and he himself got ready to go to war with demon khara. Alwar's ministers and the other people were taken aback. The reciting scholar was a skillful person. To counter this untoward situation, he calmly continued the story and said that "though all alone, Sri

Rama destroyed the army of demons and returned to Devi Sita who was waiting for Him in the Panchavati."

Hearing these words, Alwar was highly pleased and regained his composure, and ordered his army to return to capital.

Another incident of the same type:

The Ramayana scholar due to certain obligation could not come for the discourse. He deputized his son to do the discourse in his stead. His son was not aware of the King's mental condition. So, he described in detail the story of Devi Sita being abducted by demon King, Ravana. On hearing this, Alwar became so highly distressed and impatient that he shouted that 'he would go along with his army then and there, to destroy Ravana and his army and would rescue the Mother Sita, and bring her back.' He made moves to go with his army toward Lanka. His ministers judged that to reach Lanka they would have to cross over the sea- an impossibility- the King would not proceed further. But the king got down into the sea and started swimming toward Lanka. Ministers were at a loss at how to stop the King.

It is said that Sri Rama himself came to the rescue of the King Kulasekara. While the king started swimming toward Lanka, Sri Rama (accompanied by Sita and Lakshmana) appeared before Kulasekara, brought him out of the water and told him that war was over, the demons had been killed and Sita had been rescued. Sri Rama told him, 'Come, Let us all get back to your City'. Having said this, Sri Rama, Sita and Lakshmana went with Kulasekara to his city and then disappeared. While to ordinary people this story seems unbelievable, Kulasekara experienced Sri Rama's presence and intercession as real. The ministers thought that the king had gone insane. They made efforts to persuade him to return to the Kingdom in order to look after his royal duties. King awaited an opportunity to go to

"ओम् नमो नारायणाय"

॥ ஓம் நமோ நாராயணாய ॥

"*OM NAMO NARAYANAYA*"

"ओम् नमो नारायणाय"

॥ ஓம் நமோ நாராயணாய ॥

"*OM NAMO NARAYANAYA*"

the holy City of Srirangam where he wished to spend the rest of his life in the presence of Lord Sri Ranganatha in the company of Shri Vaishnavas (the devotees of Lord Narayana/Sri Ranganatha).

Ministers employed a trick to dissuade the king. They invited numerous devotees, fixing the day of invitation on the same day when the king planned to depart for Srirangam. Ministers thought that since the king was greatly attached to the Lord's devotees, he would postpone his pilgrimage. The Ministers' plan worked well. The Ministers conspired to create ill-will in the king's mind against the devotees in charge of worshipping Sri Rama in the palace temple. At the Festival time of Ramanavami, they concealed an invaluable necklace from the Rama's Murti (idol) and reported to the king that the necklace was missing. The Ministers also informed the king that only the Vaishnava devotees had freedom of movement in the palace. It followed that the necklace must have been stolen by one of the devotees.

Hearing this, the King was highly agitated, and said that the Lord's devotees could not have committed such a heinous crime. He vowed to prove what he said. As per the then prevailing tradition, the king ordered pot with a serpent in it to be brought and said that he would put his hand in the pot. If the devotees had committed this crime, the serpent in the pot would bite; otherwise the serpent would not even touch his hand. Saying this, the king put his hand in the pot and indeed was not bitten.

Witnessing this, the Ministers were ashamed of their plot and requested the king to pardon them for their crime. This story has been given by Aacharya Manakkal Nambi in the eulogistic verse at the beginning of Alwar's work "Perumal Tirumozhi".

King Kulasekara decided to abandon his kingship which he found to be full of falsehood and flaws. He enthroned his son Dridhavrata and began-as per his long-cherished desire, to live in the holy city of Srirangam, in the service and worship of Sri Ranganatha and Sri Vaishnava devotees. Additionally, he extended the third enclosure built in the Sri Ranganatha Temple which is called even today Kulasekara Veethi (Kulasekara Street or Enclosure).

The king Kulasekara went on pilgrimages to the holy places– Sri Venkata Hills (Tirupati), Chidambaram, Sri Kannapuram, Sri Vithuvakkodu, Ayodhya, etc. and after visiting these holy places, he composed 105 verses in melodious Tamil praising Lord Narayana in His Incarnations as Rama and Krishna.

The compilation of these verses is entitled "Perumal Tirumozhi". The 105 verses are divided into 10 sections. The verses describe the Alwar's self-surrender and meditative devotion to the Lord in His Incarnations as Rama and Krishna as well as His devotees and Alwar's deep desire to have the Lord's grace and to be in the company of His devotees in order to serve them.

Alwar was so devoted to Lord Narayana that he did not want to be separated from him at any point. He asked to be born and reborn on earth, particularly in the holy place Tiruvenkatam Mountain, in any form- movable or immovable, as a swan/ fish in the pond or shady groves. He wished to be steps at the entrance to the Lord's shrine on which the Lord's devotees could walk, so that he always would be in proximity to the Lord. He did not seek the attainment of heaven or (Vaikunta) emancipation or kingdom on the earth.

Alwar also announced his determination not to forsake the asylum of Lord Narayana, seated in the holy place Shri Vittuvakkodu. He sought to become a Gopi of Vrindavan in his intense eagerness to gain proximity to the Lord. He also describes becoming Devaki, the mother of Krishna whose lamentation at being separated from her child Krishna and deprivation of

''ओम् नमो नारायणाय''

|| ஓம் நமோ நாராயணாய ||

"*OM NAMO NARAYANAYA*"

the joy of raising Bala-krishna (Krishna, the child) were extremely agonizing. He also described becoming Sri Rama's mother Kaushalya, who sings a lullaby recounting major incidents in Rama's life.

Alwar also describes becoming Dasaratha, the father of Rama. Here he depicts a touching scene of the father's agony at being separated from his son Rama for 14 years. This depiction presents the deep anguish of the devotee Alwar.

At the end of this work, Alwar presents a brief Ramayana covering prominent sentimental incidents and situations beginning with the incarnation of Sri Rama and ending with the culmination of His incarnation. Alwar elaborated the final goal of the Lord's devotees, to be always at the feet of the Lord, singing His glory being immersed in devotion to him without expecting any gain.

It is also said that Kulasekara Alwar had written another work in Sanskrit entitled "Mukunda Mala"(A Garland of verses in praise of Mukunda-Lord Narayana/ Sri Ranganatha).

These Sanskrit verses describe the misery of the soul trapped in this world. The verses beseech Lord Mukunda to free the soul from the physical world.

''ओम् नमो नारायणाय''

॥ ஓம் நமோ நாராயணாய ॥

"*OM NAMO NARAYANAYA*"

Periyalwar

பெரியாழ்வார்

பெரியாழ்வாரின் திருப்பல்லாண்டின் சிறப்பை வைணவ பரம்பரையில் அறிஞர்களால் ஏற்றுக்கொள்ளப்பட்டமுறையில் ஆங்கிலத்தில் கீழே கொடுக்கப்பட்டுள்ளது .

The greatness of Alwar's work ' Tirup Pallandu ' as accepted by scholars and followed in Vaishnava tradition is given below in English .

"Periyalwar's work Tirup Pallandu (Many years of divine nature) has a significant place among the Alwar's' works of Divya Prabandham.

It is considered Pranava Mantra , that is OM, in the Vedic tradition. in the context of Veda recitation, the sacred syllable OM is chanted at the beginning and end, so Tirup Pallandu should be recited at the beginning and conclusion of the chanting of Divya Prabandham"

[Alwar's sacred work TIRUPPALLANDU]

"ओम् नमो नारायणाय"

॥ ஓம் நமோ நாராயணாய ॥

"OM NAMO NARAYANAYA"

Four

Periyalwar (Vishnuchitta) And Andal

Periyalwar, also known as Vishnuchitta, contributed to the philosophical, devotional and theological doctrines of Vaishnavism. His verses are given much importance in both the traditional patterns of daily prayers and in the rituals on festive occasions celebrated in the Vishnu/Narayana Temples. He is called Periyalwar meaning Great Alwar among all Alwars, the appellation deriving from Periyalwar's ecstatic experience on beholding the divine beauty of the Lord Narayana. Periyalwar himself blessed the Lord with safety and long life. He Is revered for his impeccable devotion to Lord Narayana.

Among the Alwar saints, Andal, the adopted daughter of Periyalwar, is the lone woman Saint having unparalleled devotion to Lord Narayana. The life of Andal embodies the eternal longing and search of the individual soul for union with the supreme soul. Andal's devotional hymns filled with love for Lord Narayana and His Incarnation as Krishna have been praised by a number of Vaishnava scholars and acharyas; noteworthy among them are Acharya Ramanuja, the founder of the Visishtadvaita system of philosophy, and acharya Sri Vedantadesika.

Periyalwar was born in a Brahmin family in the 8th century A. D. at Srivilliputtur, one of the holy cities in Tamilnadu. His father, Mukunda Bhattar and mother Padmavalli named him as Vishnuchitta, meaning the one in continuous contemplation of Lord Vishnu/Narayana or the one whom Lord Vishnu/Narayana Himself is always thinking of. The name Vishnuchitta was thus most apt since Periyalwar was a great devotee of Lord Narayana and engaged in the Lord's divine service all his life. In turn The Lord showered on him, His Grace (Anugraha) throughout his life.

Later, Vishnuchitta became popularly known as Periyalwar meaning the great Alwar.

During the later period, Periyalwar was also named by the then Pandiya King Shri Vallabhadeva as 'Bhattar Piran' meaning 'Scholar Par Excellence'. The title was bestowed by the King after witnessing Periyalwar's scholarship at the religious debate with the scholarly Pandits at the royal palace.

One night the King walked through Madurai city in disguise in order to ascertain the state of affairs in the city. When he saw someone sleeping outside a house, the king woke him and asked, "Who are you?"

The stranger said, "I am a Brahmin. I have returned from my pilgrimage to the Ganges."

The King then asked the Brahmin, "If you know something about the Dharma (ethics), please tell me."

The Brahmin in his fourfold reply said,

1. To fulfill the needs of the night, one should work during the day.
2. To fulfill the needs of the rainy season, one should work in the remaining months.
3. To fulfill the needs of the old age, one should work and make efforts in youth.

''ओम् नमो नारायणाय''

|| ஓம் நமோ நாராயணாய ||

"*OM NAMO NARAYANAYA*"

''ओम् नमो नारायणाय''

॥ ஓம் நமோ நாராயணாய ॥

"*OM NAMO NARAYANAYA*"

4. Similarly, one has to work in this life for his welfare in the next life.

On hearing this, the King began thinking that he lacked for nothing on the first three points but was at a loss for what he should do to fulfill the last Dharma, that of securing welfare in the next life. The Next day, he sent for his royal teacher Chelva Nambi and asked him, "what should I do to secure welfare in the next life?" Chelva Nambi suggested that the king arrange a debate among great scholars, on the subject of Dharma. Chelva Nambi proposed inviting scholars from the whole country. The King followed his advice and proclaimed all over the country that the scholar who would win the debate, would be awarded a bag full of gold coins. Responding to the proclamation, scholars from all over the country arrived.

Lord Narayana appearing in the dream of Periyalwar, encouraged him to participate in the debate on dharma. When Alwar, lacking the knowledge of the treatises, raised doubts about his eligibility, The Lord assured him saying that He would be with him. Thus, as directed by the Lord, Alwar went to the royal assembly and, citing proofs from the Vedas, Puranas and other treatises with the Lord's grace, proved;

"The Vaishnava dharma is the best Dharma. Lord Narayana is the supreme and the prime entity of all deities. Only 'Surrender to The Lord' (Saranagati or utter surrender to Lord Narayana) would lead the way to welfare in the next Life."

Overcome by Alwar's erudition, all the participating scholars, the King Vallabhadeva and the Royal Teacher Chelva Nambi prostrated in great reverence before the Alwar. Periyalwar received the award of a bag full of gold coins. And that is when the king Vallabhadeva bestowed upon Periyalwar the title of "Bhattar Piran"– 'Scholar Par Excellence'.

Alwar was taken in an honorific procession on an elephant through Madurai city. It is believed that Lord Narayana and His Consort Sri Devi (Goddess of Wealth) themselves appeared in the sky, seated on Garuda (mythological bird who is the vehicle of Lord Narayana) to witness the unprecedented event. Overwhelmed by the limitless beauty of the Lord, Alwar forgot his human limitation, started blessing the Lord with wellbeing through singing 'Tirup Pallandu' consisting of 12 songs invoking the Lord's long life and protection from any evil eye. Is it not surprising to see a devotee himself blessed by the Lord, blessing the Lord? Hence Alwar was called Periyalwar.

Thereafter, Periyalwar advised King Vallabhadeva to propogate Vaishnava Dharma in the entire country. He returned to Srivilliputtur, offered the prize money to be used in service to the Lord, and engaged himself in a daily routine of offering garlands to the Lord Narayana (Vatapatrasayi) in the Temple.

Periyalwar (Vishnuchitta) was married to Virajai. They had no children. Alwar was leading a calm and quiet life, maintaining a flower garden, growing beautiful flowers and Tulsi (Holy basil), used to make the garlands to adorn Lord Narayana known also as Vatapatrasayi (The Lord Who lies on the banyan leaf - Lord Vishnu or Narayana), the presiding Deity in the Temple at Srivilliputtur.

Unlike other Brahmins, Periyalwar never studied Vedic treatises. His whole life was dedicated to serving his Lord as His slave (Dasa). Ever since childhood, he was engrossed in devoted service to his Lord.

One day, while collecting flowers and Tulsi leaves in the garden, Periyalwar found a little baby girl. He took her home, named her Kodai,

''ओम् नमो नारायणाय''

॥ ஓம் நமோ நாராயணாய ॥

"*OM NAMO NARAYANAYA*"

‘‘ओम् नमो नारायणाय’’

॥ ஓம் நமோ நாராயணாய ॥

"*OM NAMO NARAYANAYA*"

meaning flower garland, and brought her up with great affection, considering her to be a gift from the Lord. From her childhood, Kodai was devoted to the Lord like her foster father. From an early age she was also known as 'Andal', which means 'one who rules over her beloved through intense devotion'. She learned to sing devotional songs by listening to her foster father and other devotee poets. Periyalwar used to tell her the stories of Lord Narayana and His incarnations, as 'Krishna' in particular. Andal listened to the spiritual and devotional discussions of her father with other saint devotees and watched them singing and dancing in trance in praise of Lord Narayana. As she grew older, her love for Lord Narayana Increased to such an extent that she started thinking of herself and behaving herself as the Lord's bride. One day Andal took the flower garland which was kept for the Lord by her father and wore it herself. She wanted to see in the mirror whether she was fit to marry the Lord Narayana, known as Sri Ranganatha, the presiding deity of the holy city Srirangam.

Father Vishnuchitta, seeing her put on the garland, became very angry and scolded her for doing such a thing. That day Vishnuchitta did not adorn his deity Sri Ranganatha with the flower Garland at all.

That same night Lord Sri Ranganatha came to him in a dream and asked Vishnuchitta 'why did not you give Me the garland today?"

Vishnuchitta replied, "My Lord! Andal made a mistake. She wore the garland herself. I did not want to bring that garland and adorn YOU."

The Lord said, "You are Mistaken. You are thinking that Andal is an ordinary human being; No, not at all. She is the Incarnation of the Earth-She is 'Bhu Devi', a divine incarnation. I wish to wear that very same garland worn by Andal."

Vishnuchitta stunned by the Lord's words, and following his instructions, adorned the Lord Sri Ranganatha with the garland worn by Andal. Thereafter Andal became known as Soodik kodutta Nacchiyar (the lady whose worn garland was used for adorning the Lord).

Vishnuchitta realized that he was blessed to have as his daughter a divine child. Andal's devotion to Sri Ranganatha grew more and more intense. She began composing songs in praise of Lord Narayana, particularly His Incarnation as Lord Krishna. These songs are well-known in Tamilnadu as Tiruppavai.

Tiruppavai songs are sung in the month of Magha. At that time also, scholars offer discourses on Andal's Tiruppavai.

In time, Andal declared that she would not marry any ordinary human being, and that she was born only for Lord Sri Ranganatha. Andal sang in ecstasy about her guiding vision of the Lord, coming in pomp and ceremony to marry her.

The father Vishnuchitta was perplexed as to how Andal's desire could be fulfilled. In this context, the Lord Sri Ranganatha Himself saved the situation by appearing in the dream of the temple priest and asking the priest to bring Andal to the temple. Andal, dressed as a bride, was brought by her father Vishnuchitta to the Temple at Srirangam.

It is said that as soon as Andal reached the deity in the sanctum, her physical form disappeared and she became one with the Lord.

For ordinary people this incident may seem incredible, but for the Sri Vaishnava devotees it is real. It may be construed as in extreme condition of Devotional Yoga (Bhakti Yoga). Andal may have reached trance state from which she never returned. The incident represents Andal's perpetual yearning, of the individual soul for union with the supreme soul, in other words her final merger with Lord Sri Ranganatha.

''ओम् नमो नारायणाय''

|| ஓம் நமோ நாராயணாய ||

"*OM NAMO NARAYANAYA*"

‘‘ओम् नमो नारायणाय’’

॥ ஓம் நமோ நாராயணாய ॥

"OM NAMO NARAYANAYA"

Thus, Vishnuchitta's daughter Andal became the consort of Sri Ranganatha; her father became the father-in-law of Lord Himself.

Vaishnava Acharya Nathamuni who compiled "Naalaayira Divya Prabandham", with the blessings of his Guru, the preceptor Nammalwar, has praised Vishnuchitta by saying "Ranganathasya swasuram" (father-in-law of Lord Sri Ranganatha), resulting in Vishnuchitta's reputation as the best of the Alwars, that is Periyalwar.

Devotional Poetic Works of Periyalwar and Andal

Periyalwar's Works :

1. Tirup Pallandu

There are two works attributed to Periyalwar; they are Tirup Pallandu and Periyalwar Tirumozhi. Some followers of Vaishnavism consider these works as two separate works, whereas others consider both works as one; i. e. Tirup Pallandu as a part of Periyalwar Tirumozhi.

The title Tirup Pallandu means 'many years of divine nature'. The occasion of this work, as explained earlier, took place when Vishnuchitta (Periyalwar), having won the religious debate at the royal palace, was honored with the title "Bhattar Piran" by the Pandiya King Sri Vallabhadeva. At that time Vishnuchitta was taken in procession on elephant and offered gold coins by the King in the presence of thousands of devotees. Wanting to see devotee Periyalwar being honored by the king, Lord Narayana with His Consort Lakshmi appeared in the sky on His vehicle Garuda. Vishnuchitta at the sight of such exquisite divine vision of Lord Narayana, fell into a trance, and in this state, 12 verses of Tirup Pallandu started flowing. These 12 verses expressed the Alwar's concern about the safety of the Lord and desire to protect him from any evil eye.

Periyalwar's Tirup Pallandu had a significant place among the Alwars' works of Divya Prabandham. It is considered Pranava Mantra, that is OM, in the Vedic tradition. As in the context of Veda- recitation, the sacred syllable OM is chanted at the beginning and end, so, Tirup Pallandu is to be recited at the beginning and conclusion of the chanting of Divya Prabandham verses, which are accepted as Tamil Veda.

For these reasons the Vaishnava acharya Manavala Mamuni (1370-1443 AD) wrote in praise of this work of Periyalwar, "is there any other work equal to Tirup Pallandu? Is there any one equal to Periyalwar?" (Upadesa Ratna Mala)

Tirup Pallandu is recited in all Vaishnava temples during daily worship.

2. Periyalwar Tirumozhi

According to scholars, Tirumozhi means holy scripture–Veda; hence Periyalwar's very important work Tirumozhi has been accepted as Veda, i.e. The Lord's Words. The second Alwar- Bhutattalwar defines Tirumozhi in his work Irandaam Tiruvantadi-Verse 64- in these words "Tirumozhiyay Ninra Tirumale" (The Veda/Tirumozhi embodies the Lord Narayana Himself).

This great work of Periyalwar consists of 461 verses in 5 cantos, which mostly depict the birth and playful childhood of Lord Krishna in Brindavan and the extreme joy of the people of Brindavan, who reveled in the divine bliss. Describing the celebratory atmosphere of Brindavan at the time of Krishna's birth, and then Krishna's childhood, Periyalwar depicts beauty of Krishna and his growth into adolescence, the influence of Krishna's flute playing on the inhabitants of Brindavan– people and animals alike, particularly the Gopis (shepherd women). He recounts many incidents from Krishna's life such as, protecting the people and cows from Lord

"ओम् नमो नारायणाय"

॥ ஓம் நமோ நாராயணாய ॥

"***OM NAMO NARAYANAYA***"

‘‘ओम् नमो नारायणाय’’

|| ஓம் நமோ நாராயணாய ||

"*OM NAMO NARAYANAYA*"

Indra's rage, by holding Govardhana mountain above their heads like an umbrella. In the process of describing Krishna's childhood, Periyalwar himself becomes Yasoda, Krishna's foster mother and immerses himself fully in Krishna consciousness.

Besides recounting the episodes about Krishna, Alwar also narrates the Lord Narayana's incarnation as Rama, describing His childhood and later the delivery of Rama's message to Sita by Hanuman while she was held captive in Lanka by demon King Ravana.

Other subjects dealt with in this treatise are as follows:

- Vaamana, Narasimha and All Other Incarnations of Lord Narayana.
- Many auspicious divine places– Tiru Maalirum cholai, Tiruk kottiyur, Deva Prayag, Srirangam and Tiru Venkatam and the presiding deity of these areas.

Additionally, Tirumozhi stresses the importance of repeatedly reciting the sacred eight-letter mantra (Ashtakshara Mantra) "OM Namo Narayanaya".

Periyalwar Tirumozhi is the essence of Alwar's devotion and self-surrender to Lord Narayana.

Andal's devotional and literary works

Andal was the only female among the twelve Alwar saints, all of whom promoted exclusive devotion to Lord Narayana. As mentioned earlier, she merged with the Lord when she entered the Sanctum Sanctorum in Srirangam Temple, decorated in bridal attire.

In her intense devotion to Lord Narayana the Saint-poet Andal started composing songs in praise of the Lord. Two literary devotional works Tiruppaavai and Naachiyaar Tirumozhi consisting of 30 and 143 verses respectively, are attributed to Andal.

ஆண்டாளின் ' நாச்சியார் திருமொழி ' ஆண்டாளின் கற்பனையை
ஆதாரமாகக் கொண்டதாகும் அந்தக்கற்பனை என்ன என்பதைக்
கீழே ஆங்கிலத்தில் கொடுக்கப்பட்டுள்ளது.

Andal
ஆண்டாள்

Andal's work 'Naachchiyaar Tirumozhi' is based on her imagination.
What was that imagination --- it is explained below in English.

**"Andal's imtense ecstatic devotion and love for
Lord Sri Ranganatha (Narayana/ Sri Krishna)
makes her imagine Srivilliputur, the place
where she lives as Brindavan, the Temple at Srivilliputtur
as the palace of Nanda- Yashoda
and her friends as the shepherd girls (Gopis) of Brindavan.
Everywhere she finds only her beloved Krishna.
"Essence of Andal's Divine Utterences:
NAACHIYAAR TIRUMOZHI**

"ओम् नमो नारायणाय"

|| ஓம் நமோ நாராயணாய ||

"*OM NAMO NARAYANAYA*"

1. Tiruppaavai

Tiruppaavai explains an important tradition of the Vaishnava religious rite, called Paavai Nombu (Vrata/Vow) practiced in the Tamil region. This Vrata is performed in the following manner :

On the full Moon day of month Magha (eleventh month in the Tamil calendar which falls between January-February) the village girls assemble at dawn on the bank of the river and worship the Goddess Devi observing the Vrata (vow), with two objectives-

1. To have good rains so that the country may prosper.
2. To get good husbands. Towards this end the village girls knock at each other's doors to awaken the girls and invite them to come to the river to observe the Vrata.

Tiruppaavai continues : Andal and her friends then go to the palace of Krishna, wake Him up and ask Him to listen to their prayers. What do they want from Him? Not wealth, or glory or even the heavenly abode Vaikunta! They merely ask that they should be born again and again to render self-less service to Him in His earthly manifestations, and to enjoy the bliss of His divine company.

As such, Andal's Tiruppaavai is the essence of Krishna worship.

It holds an important place in the tradition of Vaishnava devotion. Owing to the intensity of the worship of Lord Krishna, it's emotional majesty and literary elegance, Tiruppaavai is highly respected in Tamil Culture. Every year in the month of Magha, Tiruppaavai verses are recited in temple worship, at festivals and musical programs. Scholars of Vaishnavism are also invited to deliver discourses on Tiruppaavai.

Some examples of the high regard for Tiruppaavai are as follows:

1. Sri Ramanujacharya, used to become overwhelmed while singing the verses of Andal. Consequently, he was named as "Tiruppaavai Jeeyar", the word "Jeeyar" meaning 'Monk'; therefore "Tiruppaavai Jeeyar" means 'the Monk greatly Influenced by Tiruppaavai'.

2. Once Sri Ramanujacharya reciting the Tiruppaavai verses, reached the hermitage of his Guru Periya Nambi. At that time, he was reciting the 18th verse of Tiruppaavai which describes Nappinnai, the beloved Devi of Lord Krishna. On hearing the song, Antuzhai, the daughter of Guru Periya Nambi came out. Seeing her, Ramanujacharya fell down unconscious. Antuzhai became anxious and returning to the house told her father what had happened. Periya Nambi realizing what had occurred, consoled his daughter with these words "when Ramanuja was singing the Tiruppaavai verse concerning Devi Nappinnai, he saw you and thought that Devi herself had appeared in front of him; he was overwhelmed and fell unconscious."

3. Sri Vedantadesika, the renowned Vaishnava Acharya was greatly impressed by the deep devotion of Andal for Lord Narayana and wrote "Goda Stuti"(in Praise of Andal).

4. The 16th century Emperor of the Vijayanagara Empire Krishnadevaraya was so greatly influenced by Andal's intense Bhakti (devotion) and Prapatti (self-surrender) to the beloved Lord Narayana (Sri Ranganatha), that he wrote a poetic work in her praise, in Telugu, 'Amukta Malyada' [Amukta Malyada is the Telugu version of the Tamil "Soodik koduttha Nachchiyar" meaning the Goddess/Saintly lady- Andal who offered the garland worn by her to the Lord]

‘‘ओम् नमो नारायणाय’’

॥ ஓம் நமோ நாராயணாய ॥

"OM NAMO NARAYANAYA"

‘‘ओम् नमो नारायणाय’’

॥ ஓம் நமோ நாராயணாய ॥

"*OM NAMO NARAYANAYA*"

2. Naachiyaar Tirumozhi (Andal's Divine Utterances)

Andal as a devotee, beloved and bride of Lord Krishna, dreamt about her marriage with Lord Narayana (Lord Ranganatha). The details of her dream marriage are given in the 6th chapter of "Naachiyaar Tirumozhi". Andal, in an elaborate manner, describes her wedding with The Lord as she had seen in her dream. She describes to her girlfriend:

"Vaaranam Aayiram Soozha Valam Seithu,
Naaranan Nambi Nadakkinraan Enretir,
Poorana Porkudam Vaithup Puramenkum,
Toranam Nattak Kanaak Kanden Thozhi Naan."

("O'my friend! I saw in my dream the bridegroom Lord Narayana surrounded by a thousand beautifully decorated elephants, walking toward the specially adorned wedding pavilion, on both sides of which many people were standing carrying sacred pots filled with holy water, offering the traditional welcome to the bridegroom. The bride Andal, was extremely pleased and proud to describe her bridegroom Lord Narayana's arrival at the colorful wedding hall.")

Andal in her Tirumozhi, describes her keen desire to have Lord Sri Ranganatha as her husband, and her many efforts towards that end. She narrates to trees, creepers, flowers, sea, clouds, peacock and cuckoo the agony caused by the separation from her beloved in her hope that they will communicate her condition to the Lord so that He may come back to her.

Andal's intense ecstatic devotion and love for Lord Sri Ranganatha (Sri Krishna) makes her imagine the place where she lives, SriVilliputtur as Brindavan, the Temple at SriVilliputtur as the palace of Nanda- Yashoda and her friends as the shepherd girls (Gopis) of Brindavan. This demonstrates the presence of Krishna wherever Andal lives. Everywhere she finds only her beloved Krishna.

Nammalwar
நம்மாழ்வார்

"நாமவன் இவன் உவன் அவள் இவள் உவள் எவள்
தாமவர் இவர் உவர் அது இது உது எது
வீமவை இவை உவை அவை நலத் தீங்கவை
ஆமவை ஆய் அவை ஆய் நின்ற அவரே ! "
(திருவாய்மொழி 1/ 1/ 4)

"Naamavan Ivan uvan aval Ival uval Eval
Taamavar ivar uvar Athu Ithu Uthu Ethu
Veemavai Ivai uvai Avai Nalat Teengavai
Aamavai aay Avai aay Ninra Avare !"
(Tiruvaimozhi 1/ 1/ 4)

**" We are but He; What one says as that man and this man,
that woman and this woman, that object and this object-
all are but He, He alone .
Things with good qualities and bad qualities,
things that are at a distance, and near,
things that perish and that will come, all are He, He alone;
all define the aspects of His glory; magnificence"
TIRUVAIMOZHI (1/ 1/ 4}**

"ओम् नमो नारायणाय"

॥ ஓம் நமோ நாராயணாய ॥

"*OM NAMO NARAYANAYA*"

Five

Nammalwar (Shatagopa) & Madhura Kavi Alwar

Nammalwar (Shatagopa)

"The very first Vaishnava Acharya Nathamuni has eulogized the preeminent Alwar Nammalwar (Shatagopa), and his work Tiruvaimozhi in the following words:

"Sahasra Shakhopanishad Samaagamam"
and
"Dravida Veda Sagaram"

(Tiruvaimozhi is the Epitome of Chandogya Upanishad which itself, is the essence of Sama Veda, the ocean of Veda written in Tamil language).

Nammalwar is acclaimed as "Vedam Tamil Seitha Piran"– the author of Tamil Vedas; and Sri Nathamuni's eulogy proves Alwar's status as the foremost among the twelve Alwar Saints.

Nammalwar's disciple Madhura Kavi Alwar has written only a very small Treatise consisting of eleven verses. These verses are filled with ardent devotion to his Guru/preceptor Nammalwar.

Nammalwar belonging to the Vellala, Vaishya community, has various Names;

- Shatagopa (the one who controls the dull passions)
- Parankusa (the one whose doctrine functions like an iron hook to control the non-vedic sects other than Vaishnavism)
- Maran (the one who from birth to death does not demonstrate Worldly Nature e.g. crying, drinking milk, etc.)
- Kurukaip Piran (the Saint born in Tirukkurukur, the sacred village)
- Vedam Tamil Seitha Piran (author of the Tamil Vedas).

Nammalwar was born in the 9th century A. D. In Tirukkurukur on the bank of Tamraparni River in Tirunelveli District. This sacred place is also known as Alwar Tiru Nagari. He lived for 35 years.

Nammalwar's father was Kariyar, and his mother, Udaya Nangaiyar. The parents named their child Maran. It is believed among the Vaishnavaites that Lord Narayana or Sri Ranganatha, the presiding deity of Srirangam Shrine, Himself called him Nammalwar (Our Alwar) because He was so pleased with his Dravida Veda (Tiruvaimozhi). As a result, he became known as Nammalwar despite the many other names he carried.

At birth Nammalwar did not cry or drink milk, remaining calm and quiet. After some time, the worried parents took the child to the Vishnu Temple in the sacred village of Tirukkurukur, where they placed the child in a cradle under a tamarind tree outside the temple. Maran/Nammalwar remained by the tamarind tree for sixteen years without eating, drinking, speaking or even opening his eyes.

What transpired during that period in the life of Nammalwar, has been described by his disciple Madhura Kavi Alwar. His life sketch can be seen in detail after the eulogy of Nammalwar's four works.

''ओम् नमो नारायणाय''

॥ ஓம் நமோ நாராயணாய ॥

"*OM NAMO NARAYANAYA*"

‘‘ओम् नमो नारायणाय’’

॥ ஓம் நமோ நாராயணாய ॥

"*OM NAMO NARAYANAYA*"

The four great philosophical and theological Vaishnava treatises attributed to Nammalwar are:

Tiruviruttam; Tiruvasiriyam; Periya Tiruvantadi and Tiruvaimozhi.

Tiruvaimozhi is considered to be the treasure house of Bhakti/ devotion to Lord Narayana and philosophical knowledge. It is accepted by the Vaishnavas as greater, even, than Vedic hymns. The four works are considered as the essence of four Vedas in the following order:

- Tiruviruttam - Rigveda
- Tiruvasiriyam - Yajurveda
- Periya Tiruvantadi - Atharva Veda
- Tiruvaimozhi - Sama Veda

Tiruviruttam

This treatise consists of 100 verses and explains the Vishnu Sookta of Rigveda.

In these verses, Alwar prays to Lord Narayana to release him from worldly bondage and the cycle of Transmigration.

The first verse explains Alwar's intention.

Alwar prays to Lord Narayana on his own behalf as well as on behalf of all beings:

"O Lord Narayana who incarnates in different forms in the universe to protect all living beings! O the Master of celestial beings! Please listen to my request. Shower Your grace on all of us so as not to have the misfortune of living worldly life with this filthy body filled with ignorance, repeating the cycle of birth and death and vices".

In the concluding verse of this treatise, Alwar also asks that the chanters of these verses should not indulge in mundane worldly pleasures resulting in the cycle of birth and death, so as to attain liberation.

The remaining 98 verses describe Sringara-Bhakti i.e. Love based devotion in the Nayaka- Nayika bhava style; that is the love-based devotion between the Nayika – Nammalwar, and the beloved Nayaka – Lord Narayana.

In these verses Alwar also describes his pang of separation from the Lord and his deep desire for union with the beloved Lord. Besides, Nayika describes her agony also to her girlfriend who informs her condition to Nayaka (Lord Narayana).

Many prominent scholars – Periya Vaachaan Pillai, Azhahiya Manavala Jeeyar, Annangaracharya Swami, etc. have written profound scholarly commentaries on Tiruviruttam.

Tiruvasiriyam
(The divine Treatise composed in Tamil Asiriyappa meter)

This treatise, consisting of only seven poems, is considered to be the essence of Yajurveda.

Yajurveda has 7 sections.

A Summary of all seven sections can be seen in the Section entitled 'Narayana Sooktam' describing Lord Narayana.

As in Yajurveda, a description of Lord Narayana's abundant beauty, unlimited attributes and Supreme Power is given in the seven poems of this treatise Tiruvasiriyam.

Also explained in the last verse is Alwar's ultimate goal of Prapatti– (self-surrender) to Lord Narayana.

"Should I accept any deity inferior to, and other than, Lord Narayana?" With this question Alwar establishes his firm commitment to accept

"ओम् नमो नारायणाय"

|| ஓம் நமோ நாராயணாய ||

"*OM NAMO NARAYANAYA*"

‘‘ओम् नमो नारायणाय’’

॥ ஓம் நமோ நாராயணாய ॥

"*OM NAMO NARAYANAYA*"

servitude only to Lord Narayana, the prime cause of all celestial beings, sentient and non-sentient beings, all five elements, etc. Simultaneously, Alwar expresses his sadness for, and sympathy toward those people who not worshipping the Supreme Lord Narayana, have expressed their devotion to inferior deities with the aim of obtaining selfish benefits. In so doing, they remain drowned in the ocean of worldly sorrows and difficulties and entrenched in the cycle of birth and death.

In summary, Tiruvasiriyam presents Alwar's goal of self-surrender to the Lord in a narrative of devotion to Lord Narayana rather than striving for moksha (liberation).

Periya Tiruvantadi

"Periya Tiruvantadi", the third Treatise of Nammalwar consisting of 87 verses is presented as an interpretation of Mundaka and other Upanishads. It is considered to be the essence of Atharva Veda.

Most of the verses in this Treatise are in praise of the attributes of Lord Narayana. In the very first verse, Alwar reflects on the attributes, beauty of and service to Lord Narayana. He requests his own thoughts to focus on the Lord so that he can worship Him through his poetic verses. In the last verse Alwar advises his own mind and those of all human beings to worship at the feet of Lord Narayana, to chant and meditate on His auspicious names in order to enable liberation from their sins. Thus, we find Alwar's deep devotion to Lord Narayana being elucidated in both the first and last verses of this treatise. The object of the whole treatise is Alwar's assertion that the only way to get rid of all our material/ physical problems and sins, is to devote ourselves to Lord Narayana.

Nammalwar considers that :

"Lord Narayana's Grace alone, is responsible for his Bhakti and Prapatti.
He alone draws the devotee towards Him;
He alone showers abundant love on him like a mother;
He alone fulfills his well-being like a father and
He alone shows right path like a teacher.
(Verse 5)

The entire treatise is filled with the description of the power of devotion; surrender at the Feet of the Lord; meditation on and chanting of the Lord's attributes and names. According to Alwar, the bliss derived from these endeavors is many times greater than the Aananda (Bliss) achieved from attaining 'Vaikuntta' (Lord's abode).
(Verse 53)

Tiruvaimozhi
(The Lord's Divine Words – Tamil Veda)

According to Nathamuni, the very first Acharya among the Vaishnava Acharyas, Nammalwar's Tiruvaimozhi is "Dravida Veda Sagara" (the ocean of Veda composed in Tamil language). In his Sanskrit Eulogy to this divine work, Nathamuni states :

"Aham Shri- Shatagopa—vaanmayam,
Dravida–veda–sagaram Namaami"

(I offer my Salutations to Sri Shatagopa's treatise Tiruvaimozhi, the ocean of Tamil Veda)

Another Vaishnava Acharya, Bhattar, in his Eulogy says "Shatagopa is the mother who gave birth to Tamil Veda Tiruvaimozhi, having more than 1000 verses which describe the divine attributes of grace, kindness, etc. and that Sri Ramanuja, the founder of the philosophic system of Visishtadvaita,

''ओम् नमो नारायणाय''

|| ஓம் நமோ நாராயணாய ||

"*OM NAMO NARAYANAYA*"

''ओम् नमो नारायणाय''

|| ஓம் நமோ நாராயணாய ||

"*OM NAMO NARAYANAYA*"

is its foster mother". Sri Ramanuja propagated this Tamil Veda extensively and Vaishnavites accepted Tiruvaimozhi as the most important base for Sri Ramanuja's Sri Bhashya.

Tiruvaimozhi is also a treasure house of emotional, sentimental, devotional and blissful literature.

In addition to the descriptions of Lord Narayana's magnificent beauty, manifold attributes and grace towards His devotees, it elaborately extolls Narayana's avataras (incarnations) and their Leelas (acts) for the protection of the universe.

In verses 1,2,3,6, 7 and 10 in Decad 7. Section 4, Alwar describes the features of different incarnations- Vamana, Kurma, Varaha, Narasimha, Rama, and Krishna Avataras.

Vamana : Alwar was astonished to see the mighty Lord taking the small form of Brahmin Vamana (dwarf) and coming before King Bali who had been terrorizing the universe. During the period of his Yagya (sacrifice) Vamana asked three steps of earth as dakshina (gift to a Brahmin). On being promised by King Bali, the Lord assumed a mighty form measuring the whole universe in two steps. As there was no terrain to accommodate the third step, the Lord put His foot on Bali's head sending him to Patala Loka (the region below the earth), thus, saving the universe from King Bali's atrocities. "What a beautiful mighty and astonishing dwarf form the Lord has taken, and Alwar has extolled!".
(Verse 1)

Kurma : Verse 2 narrates the story of Lord Narayana's Incarnation as tortoise (Kurma) during the period of Amruta mantanam (Churning of the milky ocean) for the purpose of drawing out nectar to protect the Devas (celestial beings) and the universe from the asuras (demons).

When the Meru mountain, being used to churn the milky ocean, started to move, Lord Narayana took the form of a huge tortoise and carried the mountain on His back thus stabilizing the Meru mountain. "What a gigantic form as a tortoise Lord Narayana had taken for saving creation, etc…..!" (Verse 2)

Varaha : In the incarnation of Varaha Avatara (incarnation as a huge boar/ wild pig) "he speared the earth along with all beings and elements on his tusk. In the ocean he fought with the demon Hiranyaksha and killed him and in so doing assured the protection of the earth and all creations (seven worlds, seven mountains and seven oceans) from the demon's clutches." (Verse 3)

Narasimha : Lord Narayana took the form of Narasimha (Half man-Half lion) in order to protect His devotee Prahlada from the atrocities of Prahlada's demon father Hiranyakashipu. "What a frightening scene it was, Lord Narayana tearing open the chest of the demon with His claws!". Verse 6

Rama & Krishna : Verses 7 and 10 in Section 4 in decad 7 chronicle the following respectively:

- The devastation of war in Lanka between the Lord incarnated as Rama and the demon king Ravana.
- Wonderful description of Lord Krishna holding Govardhana mountain to protect the people of Gokul from the fiery rain brought forth by angry Indra, the master of celestial beings.

Nammalwar's Tiruvaimozhi consisting of 1102 verses (Hymns), as stated earlier, has been accepted by Vaishnava saints and scholars as the supreme Tamil Veda the equivalent to Sama Veda.

Vaishnava Acharya Manavala Mamuni (1370- 1443 A. D.) best-known after Ramanuja in the lineage of Vaishnava Saints and Teachers proves in

‘‘ओम् नमो नारायणाय’’

|| ஓம் நமோ நாராயணாய ||

"*OM NAMO NARAYANAYA*"

''ओम् नमो नारायणाय''

॥ ஓம் நமோ நாராயணாய ॥

"OM NAMO NARAYANAYA"

his creation 'Tiruvaimozhi Nootrantadi' – 100 verses composed in praise of Tiruvaimozhi that 'Tiruvaimozhi' is equivalent to Sama veda.

In the first verse of this work Mamuni explains that Tiruvaimozhi expounds the Supreme Upanishadic "Neti, Neti" (Endless) principle of the All- pervasiveness of Lord Narayana.

The later Vaishnava Acharya Vedanta Desika (13th- 14th centuries) also had declared Tiruvaimozhi as the greatest Tamil Veda:

"Arumaraihal Tamil seithaan Taale Kondu"
(By taking refuge at the holy feet of Nammalwar who composed the greatest Vedas in Tamil.........)

Tiruvaimozhi is considered as the essence of Sama Veda because of two special features; One feature is that the verses of Tiruvaimozhi are set in melodious tunes that can be sung like Mantras of Sama Veda. The second feature is that Tiruvaimozhi expounds the philosophical principle of 'Ultimate Brahman', as extolled in the Sama Veda.

This Dravida Veda has been accepted as the summary of the spiritual principle extolled in Chandogya Upanishad. It has been stated by Acharya Nathamuni in His Sanskrit Eulogy to Tiruvaaimozhi:

"Sahasra-Shakhopanishad Samaagamam"– "summary of the Chandogya Upanishad, having thousands of branches" – in brief, the essence of Sama Veda.

The entire Tiruvaimozhi defines the divine experience of Alwar, a staunch devotee of Lord Narayana – by describing the

- soul's (Alwar) enduring pain at its separation from the Lord.
- soul's surrender to the Lord.
- the experience of soul becoming one with the Lord.

In verse 4 in the first decad of Tiruvaimozhi, the Vedic principle of the All-pervasiveness of Brahman in Lord Narayana is proven.

Verse 4 :

"We are but He. What one says as that man and this man, that woman and this woman, that object and this object – all are but He, He alone. Things with good qualities and bad qualities, that are at a distance, and near, things that perish and that will come, all are He, He alone; all define the aspects of His glory; magnificence."

Nammalwar's Tiruvaimozhi is the essence of the Divine Truth of Chandogya Upanishad (the fundamental theme of Sama Veda) –"Sarvam Khalvidam Brahma" -all are but Brahman - the inward meaning being "all active and inactive beings are but He, that is Brahman/ Lord Narayana. The universe composed of the five elements – Earth, Water, Fire, Wind and Sky, is He and all traits of the elements are His features."

(decad 1 Section 1).

The decad 10, Section 5, Verse 3 describes the summary of the Alwar's Tamil Veda.

"Lord Narayana creates the whole universe by Himself without any help, and protects everything from the deluge (Pralaya) Himself.

The same section explains the path of devotion to Lord Narayana by "worshipping Him with fresh flowers, chanting and singing the Lord's divine names e.g. Madhava, surrendering at the Lord's feet, praising the Lord and His divine abode Tiru Venkatam mountain, etc......".

Madhura Kavi Alwar

Madhura Kavi Alwar was born into a Brahmin family in the holy place called Tirukkolur near Alwar Tirunagari in the 9th century A.D. before his

''ओम् नमो नारायणाय''

|| ஓம் நமோ நாராயணாய ||

"OM NAMO NARAYANAYA"

"அன்னையாய் அத்தனாய் என்னை ஆண்டிடும்
தன்மையான் சடகோபன் என் நம்பியே" பாசுரம் 4
"தேவு மற்று அறியேன் குருகூர் நம்பி" பாசுரம் 2
".......குருகூர் நம்பிக்கு ஆள்
உரியனாய் அடியேன் பெற்ற நன்மையே !" பாசுரம் 3
(கண்ணிநுண் சிருத்தாம்பு)

"Annaiyay attanaay ennai aandidum
Tanmaiyan sadagopan en Nambiye" Paasuram 4
"Tevu matru ariyen kurukur. Nambi " Paasuram 2
" ......" Kurukur Nambikku aaal
Uriyanaay Adiyen Petra Nambiye !"
(Kanninun Siruttambu)

"Madhura Kavi Alwar accepted his Guru/ preceptor
Nammalwar as the adorable Lord
and the devotion to Him
as the essence of his whole life
and only by the grace of Guru,
the path of devotion to Lord Narayana would open up."
Essence of Alwar's work:
(KANNINUN SIRUTTAMBU)

Madhura Kavi Alwar

மதுர கவி ஆழ்வார்

preceptor (spiritual Guru) Nammalwar. He is believed to have learned all the Sanskrit Vedas and to have mastery over Sanskrit and Tamil.

He was not interested in worldly attractions even from an early age. He was interested in only Narayana Bhakti (Devotion to Lord Narayana), i.e. towards the spiritual way of life. Madhur Kavi Alwar undertook a pilgrimage to the divine places in North India–Ayodhya, Gaya, Badri and Dwaraka among them. One night, having reached Ayodhya, he noticed a luminous ball of fire in the sky slowly moving toward the South.

He tried to understand what it was, but could not do so. He decided to follow that fireball and moved towards southern India. This lead him to the holy place of Tirukkurukur where the glow of fire disappeared.

Madhura Kavi went around the holy place making enquiries, as to whether anything special was happening. There, at last he learned that a sixteen-year-old boy (Nammalwar) had been sitting under a tamarind tree by the Temple since his birth, eating nothing and emitting a divine glow.

Madhura Kavi then went to the temple and saw Nammalwar sitting still, in state of Samadhi with eyes closed. In order to ascertain whether the boy was alive, he picked up a stone and let it drop. On hearing the sound of that stone, the boy opened his eyes and smilingly looked at Madhura Kavi. In an effort to learn whether the boy could speak, Madhura Kavi asked him a question.

"If the 'small' (Soul) inhabits a dead body, what will it eat and where will it remain?"

Meaning of the question was:

If the subtle soul enters the gross mortal body then,

- What will it eat,

''ओम् नमो नारायणाय''

॥ ஓம் நமோ நாராயணாய ॥

"*OM NAMO NARAYANAYA*"

"ओम् नमो नारायणाय"

॥ ஓம் நமோ நாராயணாய ॥

"OM NAMO NARAYANAYA"

- What will it experience,
- And where will it remain.

Responding to this question Nammalwar broke his silence, "It will eat that and will rest there" Meaning of the Nammalwar's response:

- The Soul will remain in the mortal body,
- Experience the happiness and the sadness arising from the senses
- and remains confined to the same body.

On hearing this philosophic truth Madhura Kavi fell at the feet of Nammalwar, becoming his disciple and serving him for the remainder of his life- about nineteen years.

Thereafter, Madhura Kavi compiled and codified all of the literary philosophic verses of his Preceptor Nammalwar, composed tunes to all the verses and recited them devotedly, popularizing them all over South India.

Even today, if we take pride in having intact the great Tamil Veda of Nammalwar, Tiruvaimozhi (1102 Verses), it is only because of Madhura Kavi's devotion to his Guru (Aacharya Bhakti) and his dedication to the compilation of Nammalwar's works –Tiru Viruttam; Tiruvaasiriyam; Periya Tiruvantadi and Tiruvaimozhi.

After the Samadhi of his Guru Nammalwar, the disciple Madhura Kavi spent rest of his own life eulogizing his preceptor by singing his verses. He arranged for a Temple to be built at Tirukkurukur, the birth place of Nammalwar, had Nammalwar's idol installed in the Temple and made arrangements for its continuous worship.

In Madhur Kavi's era, like the old Tamil Sangams, the Academy of scholars existed in Madurai under the patronage of Pandya King. Traditionally, any type of literature could get popularized in the society only with the sanction of the Academy (Sangam). When the members of the Sangam learned that

Madhura Kavi had been reciting the verses of glorious tales and works of Nammalwar, the Sangam asked Madhura Kavi to present a sample of these to them so that they could evaluate their worth. Madhura Kavi presented the following verse from Tiruvaimozhi, written on a palm leaf to the Sangam.

"Kannan Kazhalinai Nannum Manamudaiyeer!
Ennum Tirunaamam Tinnam Naaraname! (10/ 5/ 1)

Meaning: Ye men seeking asylum at the feet of Lord Krishna! The Sacred Name Narayana alone, is worthy of meditation; no other name!

The Tamil Sangam's tradition for evaluating a literary work was as follows.

The literary works received for evaluation were placed on planks and subsequently set to float in the lotus pond of Madurai Temple. The best of them remain afloat on the plank, while the rest would sink.

When the Sangam followed this tradition to evaluate the work of Nammalwar, the palm leaf containing Nammalwar's verse remained afloat. After this the Sangam recognized the works of Nammalwar as the best of that period. Scholars and commoners alike recognized the high quality of Nammalwar's works.

Madhura Kavi Alwar also wrote a literary and devotional work entitled "Kanninun Siruttambu" consisting of 11 verses presenting a glorious eulogy to his preceptor Nammalwar. This work was incorporated in the Divya Prabandham.

While entire Divya Prabandham is focused on devotion to Lord Narayana, His incarnations and the dignity of Narayana worship, Madhura Kavi's divine verses underscore the greatness of the preceptor and the disciple's devotion to the Guru. Although the work of Madhura Kavi consists of only 11 verses, it remains highly regarded by scholars.

''ओम् नमो नारायणाय''

॥ ஓம் நமோ நாராயணாய ॥

"*OM NAMO NARAYANAYA*"

‘‘ओम् नमो नारायणाय’’

॥ ஓம் நமோ நாராயணாய ॥

"OM NAMO NARAYANAYA"

Vaishnavism holds the view that a pupil obtains a preceptor through the Lord's grace and that one can approach the Lord through the kindness of the preceptor; as such Guru is greater than even the Lord.

Madhura Kavi Alwar's work "Kanninun Siruttambu" starts with the story of Bala Krishna (child Krishna) being tied with a rope by his mother Yashoda as his punishment for roaming around Vrindavan to steal milk/ butter collected by shepherd girls (Gopis). There are no poems on worship of Krishna. Instead, Madhur Kavi's work expresses the essence of devotion and surrender to his Guru Nammalwar, whose hundreds of poems propounded his own deep devotion to Lord Krishna (Narayana).

In his work–Upadesa Ratnamala Vaishnava Saint Manavaala Mamuni (1370-1443) eulogized the Madhura Kavi's work (Kanninun Siruttambu) in the following words:

"The great Alwar saints have included this literary work of Madhura Kavi, which presents the essence of Guru Bhakti (Devotion to the divine teacher) in the great divine scholarly work 'Naalaayira Divya Prabandham' (4000 Divine Verses of Alwars)".

The great Vaishnava Acharya and Philosopher Vedanta Desika of the 13th /14th century has said in praise of Madhura Kavi:

"Madhura Kavi experienced ecstatic pleasure in surrendering himself at the feet of his Guru Nammalwar, the author of Tamil Veda Tiruvaimozhi. The holy path of devotion to the preceptor shown by Madhura Kavi is the purest path for the seekers of the spiritual path."

In "Kanninunun Siruttambu" Madhura Kavi says, "uttering the name of the preceptor provides one's tongue nectar like the sweetest and most blissful experience". For Madhur Kavi Alwar, the most revered Guru Nammalwar was the only Lord; he asserts that he knows only his preceptor Nammalwar as the adorable Lord. Madhura Kavi accepted

"Guru Bhakti" as the essence of his whole life. He fully believed that only by the grace of the preceptor, the Path of Narayana Bhakti (The path of devotion to Lord Narayana) would open up.

Vaishnava Acharya Scholar Nathamuni (9th century) compiler of the Naalaayira Divya Prabandham, prayed Madhura Kavi, "Let Madhura Kavi who does not know anything other than devotion to His Guru Nammalwar and who accepts Nammalwar alone as his master, dwell in my mind all the time".

Sri Vaishnava Acharyas Parasara Bhattar, Nampillai, and Periyavaachaan Pillai have commented upon Madhura Kavi's work as well.

According to the Sri Vaishnava tradition, while worshipping Lord Narayana, scholars used to recite Nammalwar's Tiruvaimozhi, the Tamil Veda continuously. Also, they would recite Madhura Kavi Alwar's "Kanninun Siruttambu" at the beginning as well as at the end of the recital. This auspicious tradition is followed even today.

''ओम् नमो नारायणाय''

|| ஓம் நமோ நாராயணாய ||

"*OM NAMO NARAYANAYA*"

"திரு மரு மார்வ ! நின்னைச் சிந்தையுள் திகழ் வைத்து
மருவிய மனத்தராகில் மாநிலத்து உயிர்கள் எல்லாம்

....

அருவினைப் பயன் அது உய்யார் அரங்கமா நகருளானே !
(திருமாலை , பாசுரம் 40)

....

இழி குலத்தவர்களேலும் எம் அடியார்கள் ஆகில்

....

வழிபட அருளினாய் போல் மதிள் திரு அரங்கத்தானே !"
(திருமாலை, பாசுரம் 42)

"Tiru Maru Maarva ! Ninnaich chintaiyul tikazhavaittu
Maruviya manattharaakil maanilattu uyirkal Ellam
Aruvinaip payan Athu Uyyaar Arangama nakarulane !
(Tirumaalai ; Verse. 40)

....

Izhi kulatthavarkalelum Em adiyaarkal. aakil

....

Vazhipada arulinaay pol Mathil Tiru Arangattaane ! "
(Tirumaalai; Verse 42)

**[Alwar believes] " Even the greatest sinners
would be absolved of all their sins,
If they are immersed in devotion to
Lord Narayana (Sri Ranganatha),
continuously meditate on Him, taking refuge in Him."
Alwar considers the Lord's devotees as the
Lord Himself and as He is adored, so should they be."
TIRUMAALAI (The DIVINE GARLAND OF SONGS) - Verses 40 & 42**

Tondaradippodi Alwar

தொண்டரடிப்பொடியாழ்வார்

Six

Tondaradippodi Alwar (Vipra Narayana)

A well-known saying among the Vaishnava devotees about the sacred Garland of divine songs 'Tirumaalai' composed by Tondaradippodi Alwar is, "Tirumaalai Ariyaathaar Tirumaalai Ariyaathaare", meaning those who do not know the Alwar's devotional work Tirumaalai, do not know Lord Narayana (Tirumaal– Lord Narayana).

Tondaradippodi Alwar has sang the eulogy of the holy place Srirangam and the Presiding Deity of that divine place, Sri Ranganatha in his Book of hymns 'Tirumaalai'. It is not an exaggeration to regard Tirumaalai as "Sriranga Maahaatmya"– A work celebrating the greatness of Srirangam and Sri Ranganatha.

In his work Prabandha Saaram, the renowned Vaishnava Acharya Sri Vedantadesika has sung in praise of Tondaradippodi Alwar's both works– 'Tirumaalai' and 'Tirup Palli Ezhuchchi', in the following words:

"Tunnu pukazht Tondaradippodiye!
Adiyenukku Arul Chey parinthu neeye!"

''ओम् नमो नारायणाय''

|| ஓம் நமோ நாராயணாய ||

"*OM NAMO NARAYANAYA*"

“ओम् नमो नारायणाय”

॥ ஓம் நமோ நாராயணாய ॥

"*OM NAMO NARAYANAYA*"

"'O' eminent and famed Tondaradippodi! You have showered your grace on me (the servant of Sri Ranganatha) by creating these two-sacred works!"

Among the 12 Tamil Vaishnava saints Tondaradippodi Alwar is well-known for his works – 'Tirup palli Ezhuchchi' (songs to awaken the Lord Narayana in the early morning) and 'Tirumaalai' (Garland of 45 songs filled with devotion and self-surrender to the Lord).

Tondaradippodi Alwar, on being born was named as Vipra Narayana. He was born in the 8th century A.D. in a Vaishnava Brahmin family in Tirumandankudi Village near Kumbhakonam in Tanjore District in Tamilnadu. He became well-known as Tondaradippodi Alwar. The name Tondaradippodi Alwar means, Alwar who carries on his head the dust of the feet of the Lord's devotees.

His whole life was dedicated to the service and devotion to Lord Narayana and to the service of His devotees. Following the family tradition, he studied the Vedas and Shastras. He was not interested in family life; he followed the life of a Brahmachari i.e. the celibate life, deciding to lead his life in the service of the Lord. He reached the holy place of Srirangam where he made flower garlands to decorate Lord Narayana laying on the 'Adisesha' bed in the Temple. For this purpose, he created a flower garden cultivating various kinds of fragrant flowers. He lived in a hut in the garden itself where he resided happily living on the alms he received from the families in Srirangam.

During this period, a sudden turn took place in his life. He became attracted to a beautiful woman named Devadevi and for some time forgot the devotional and spiritual duties. He became entangled in the life of worldly enjoyment and faced various problems attendant on this entanglement. Eventually, with the grace of the Lord, he realized the impermanence of worldly enjoyments and the problems associated with the duality of worldly existence. Gradually he got over the attraction to Devadevi and rededicated himself to Lord Sri Ranganatha's worship and service to the Lord's devotees.

It is believed that Devadevi also repented her involvement in the worldly life of desires and pleasures, and changed her own life, leading an ordinary and simple life.

The outstanding quality of Alwar was his dedicated service to the devotees of Lord Sri Ranganatha. According to him, to whatever caste the devotee may belong, he is worshippable. As such if a person belonging to higher caste, insults a devotee born into a lower caste, the former will be considered low. The Lord loves his devotee born into a lower caste, more than even a Brahmin possessing Vedic scholarship.

A brief introduction to these two treatises:

1) Tirup palli Ezhuchchi is a collection of 10 songs which Alwar sang to awaken the Lord Sri Ranganatha. Through these songs, Alwar describes the natural beauty of early morning.

"Sun has risen, Darkness has ceased,
Various flowers have blossomed; Birds are singing;
A Sweet wind is blowing;
Shepherds are going to the forest for their cows, calves to graze."

There Alwar prays to the Lord to awaken and shower His grace on His devotees who have been awaiting his protection from the effects of evil. Alwar also submits that the celestial beings including singers, musicians and dancers are waiting for the Lord to awaken so that through their music, dance, instruments and flower offerings, they can worship Him.

Although small in size, this Book of 10 songs, remains a treasure trove of devotion and surrender to the Lord.

''ओम् नमो नारायणाय''

|| ஓம் நமோ நாராயணாய ||

"OM NAMO NARAYANAYA"

''ओम् नमो नारायणाय''

॥ ஓம் நமோ நாராயணாய ॥

"*OM NAMO NARAYANAYA*"

2) The second Book Tirumaalai is composed of 45 songs, the sacred garlands of hymns in praise of the Lord Sri Ranganatha. The title of the Book itself means "The Divine Garland of Songs".

As said earlier, among Vaishnava devotees, common saying is: "Tirumaalai Ariyaathaar Tirumaalai Ariyaathaare!" which means, "Those who do not know Tirumaalai" (Alwar's work), do not know Lord Narayana". (Tirumaal means Lord Vishnu or Narayana or Sri Ranganatha and Tirumaalai is the title of Alwar's book meaning Divine Garland of Songs).

Alwar's songs describe the grace of Lord Ranganatha, the power of chanting the Lord's divine names and devotees' helplessness in the world of contrasts where only the Lord is refuge. Alwar's songs voice his sadness at not being bestowed with the vision of the Lord and in the same breath they describe the greatness of the devotees. Alwar believes that even if the Lord's devotee is born into a lower caste, and commits sinful acts, he will be considered as equal to a person of high caste as a result of his 'Prapatti' (deepest devotion/surrender to the Lord).

In this context, the following songs are noteworthy.

Alwar sings :

'O' Lord! You are the prime cause, during the 'Pralaya' the deluge, you saved and protected the three worlds inside Your stomach and then brought them out at the beginning of creation.

'O' Lord! the presiding deity of the great city of Srirangam! We learned the chanting of Your divine names from the great saints, resulting in control of our senses and removal of all our sins; we thus conquered sinful life, not allowing the messengers of Yama, God of death (Yama dutas), to gain proximity and take away our lives.

(song 1)

Alwar's song 2 explains that in comparison to the joy derived from the chanting of the Lord's names, the joy derived from obtaining even Vaikuntta pales.

'O' Lord Narayana / Sri Ranganatha residing in the holy city of Srirangam for the benefit of the common people! O' the Lord of Devas! 'O' the Lord Achyuta staying in the hearts of devotees! I enjoy supreme bliss and joy by chanting Your sweet divine names; Compared to this joy, I don't wish to experience even the enjoyment of heaven.

(song 2)

Alwar's assertion is that the joy a devotee derives from chanting the divine names is incomparable. And he would not even desire the attainment of Moksha (liberation from worldly material life).

According to Alwar, divine service is important, but more important still is service to the Lord's devotees, irrespective of the caste into which they were born. In the song 39 Alwar says, "Lord Sri Ranganatha is more pleased with those who though born into a lower caste, offer divine service and remain deeply devoted to the Lord, than those who are born into higher caste – Brahmins, well versed in all four Vedas; but do not consider the service to Lord Sri Ranganatha as their supreme goal of lives.

Tondaradippodi Alwar, true to his name, (Alwar who carries on his head the dust of the feet of the Lord's devotees) puts greater credence in devotion and service to the Divine than caste or knowledge of the Vedas and shastras.

Alwar opines:

"If a person is born into a higher caste and is well versed in scriptures, but is not a devotee, and does not do service to the Lord, He, the Lord will not be pleased with that person."

(song 39)

''ओम् नमो नारायणाय''

॥ ஓம் நமோ நாராயணாய ॥

"*OM NAMO NARAYANAYA*"

" கொண்டல் வண்ணனைக் கோவலனாய் வெண்ணெய்
உண்டவாயன் என்னுள்ளம் கவர்ந்தானை
அண்டர்கோன் அணியரங்கன் என்னமுதினைக்
கண்ட கண்கள் மற்றொன்றினைக் காணாவே ! "
(அமலன் ஆதி பிரான் பாசுரம் 10)

" Kondal vannanaik kovalanaay vennai
Undavaayan ennullam kavarntaanai
Andarkon Aniyarangan ennamuthinaik
Kanda Kankal matronrinaik Kaanaave ! "
(Amalan Aadi Piraan; Verse 10)

**"KONDAL VANNANAI ....KANDA KANKAL
MATRONRINAIK KAANAAVE !"**
**"Having had the divine vision of
Lord Narayana whose color
Is like a dark cloud;
what further is there to be seen !!
[it implies that nothing else remained to be seen !]"**

(AMALAN ADI PIRAAN- Verse 10)

Tiruppan Alwar
திருப்பாணாழ்வார்

Alwar also believes that if immersed in devotion to Lord Narayana, continuously meditating on Sripati Narayana (Sri Ranganatha) and taking refuge in Him, even the greatest sinners would be absolved of all their sins.

Alwar considers the Lord's devotees as the Lord Himself and as He is adored, so should they be.

(song 42)

''ओम् नमो नारायणाय''

|| ஓம் நமோ நாராயணாய ||

"*OM NAMO NARAYANAYA*"

‘‘ओम् नमो नारायणाय’’

॥ ஓம் நமோ நாராயணாய ॥

"*OM NAMO NARAYANAYA*"

Seven

Tiruppan Alwar

The Vaishnava saint-devotee Tiruppan Alwar belonged to the 8th century; he was raised by a family of Paanar in Uraiyur village in Trichy District in Tamilnadu. It is believed that a Paanar couple, who had no children, found the child in a grain field; brought him home and raised the child happily. Since it was a Paanar couple who raised the child, he became known as Paanan; Later he became a staunch devotee of the Lord Sri Ranganatha, the presiding deity of the well-known Srirangam Temple, situated very close to his village Uraiyur on the bank of holy Cauvery River; hence he became Tiruppaan Alwar.

At that time the Paanar caste was considered to be one of the lowest castes. The people of this caste were great 'Veena' musicians (string instrument) but they were not allowed to enter the temples. From childhood Paanan became an expert in playing Veena. He was not interested in worldly life, but deeply interested in devotion to Lord Narayana (Sri Ranganatha), from the very early stages of his life. Subject to the traditions of the time, Paanan could not go into the Temple. Standing in Cauvery river itself, facing the Lord in the temple, Paanan was immersed in devotion to Lord Sri Ranganatha, continuously playing the Veena for Him and singing His praises. Sometimes, in utter devotion to Lord Sri Ranganatha, Paanan would lose consciousness as he sang the glories of the Lord accompanied by his Veena.

One day, a miracle happened. Paanan, completely immersed in devotion to the Lord, was standing in Cauvery River, singing in an ecstatic state. At that moment, the Srirangam Temple Priest Yogi Loka Sarang, who belonged to a Brahmin caste, came there to fetch water for bathing the idol of Sri Ranganatha as part of the daily worship. The priest tried to attract the attention of Paanan to give way to him, but Paanan in his ecstatic state could not hear him. Others also tried to wake him up from the state of ecstasy. The priest went so far as to pick a stone and throw it at him. The stone hit Paanan's head and blood flowed all over his face. When Paanan came to his senses, afraid, he apologized to the priest and everyone and ran from the place.

When the priest Loka Sarang came to the Temple to bathe the Lord, he saw blood flowing from the Lord's face. The news of this spread far and wide. Because of the incident the priest was greatly worried. At night, Lord Sri Ranganatha appeared to Loka Sarang in dream. The Lord made the priest understand that he had committed a great sin by insulting His devotee, Paanan. The Lord told Loka Sarang to carry Paanan on his shoulders to His Sanctum Sanctorum in the temple. The dream relieved Loka Sarang of his worry. He informed the officials of the Temple of the Lord's instruction and sent word to Paanan, inviting him to follow the Lord's command.

Since he belonged to lowest caste, Paanan was hesitant, but Loka Sarang repeated Lord's instructions as given in his dream. Finally, Paanan agreed. The priest carried Paanan to the inner shrine of the Temple where Paanan, looking at the extreme beauty of his Lord from feet to head, became ecstatic and sang 10 songs starting with the words "Amalan Aadi Piran" (Pure, Prime and Great Lord) which became the title of Tiruppan Alwar's book. Paanan, in ecstasy, having gained the experience of being at the feet of the Lord and imbibing His beauty, presented that divine experience for

‘‘ओम् नमो नारायणाय’’

|| ஓம் நமோ நாராயணாய ||

"*OM NAMO NARAYANAYA*"

''ओम् नमो नारायणाय''

|| ஓம் நமோ நாராயணாய ||

"*OM NAMO NARAYANAYA*"

the benefit of others through his songs. On having this experience Paanan said

"What else would I like to see in the world?" implying that nothing else remained to be seen or enjoyed. [Song 10].

It is believed that after uttering these words, Paanan in his ecstasy became one with the Lord; that is, he merged into the image of Lord Sri Ranganatha.

Although Paanan belonged to the lowest caste, his deep devotion to Lord Sri Ranganatha bestowed upon him the honor of being Alwar. Subsequently he became known as Tirup Paan Alwar. Since Yogi and Sage-like priest Loka Sarang carried the devotee Paanan to Lord Sri Ranganatha, Paanan was called Yogivah and Munivah (he who was carried by Yogi/Muni Loka Sarang) in Sanskrit.

This episode teaches that Sri Vaishnava devotees may belong to even the lowest caste; however, if they are great devotees of Lord Sri Ranganatha, they must be worshipped even by people of higher caste and great vedic scholarship.

Amalan Adi Piraan, consisting of 10 songs espouses the divine qualities of Lord Narayana/Sri Ranganatha. These 10 songs describe the unparalleled beauty of the Lord in the following order:

"Alwar, while having the divine vision of the Lord, ecstatically begins His description with the Lord's holy feet, His attractive dress–Pitambar, the Lotus flower in His navel, His belt, broad chest where Lakshmi, his consort and the Goddess of wealth resides, His red lips and eyes thus, constituting the extremely beautiful form of Sri Ranganatha and Alwar's blissful experience. Alwar's eyes are filled with the beauty of the Lord and his own ecstatic joy".

" குலம் தரும் செல்வம் தந்திடும் அடியார்
படுதுயர் ஆயின எல்லாம்
நிலந்தரம் செய்யும் நீள் விசும்பு அருளும்
அருளொடு பெருநிலம் அளிக்கும்
பலம் தரும் மற்றும் தந்திடும் பெற்ற
தாயினும் ஆயின செய்யும்
நலம் தரும் சொல்லை நான் கண்டுகொண்டேன்
நாராயணா என்னும் நாமம் !"
(பெரிய திருமொழி ; பாசுரம் 1 / 1 / 9)

" Kulam Tarum selvam tanthidum adiyaar
Padutuyar Aayina Ellam
Nilantaram seyyum neel visumbu arulum
Arulodu perunilam alikkum
Balam Tarum matrum tanthidum Petra
Taayinum Aayina seyyum
Nalam Tarum sollai Naan kandu konden
Narayana ennum Naamam ! "
(Periya Tirumozhi ; Verse 1 / 1 / 9)

ALWAR believes:

"The holy name of Narayana
is the harbinger of all great things,
such as power, noble family and wealth,
and eliminates sorrows of the devotee;
I found all good things by
chanting the sacred name of Narayana "
PERIYA TIRUMOZHI 1/1/9

Tirumangai Alwar

திருமங்கை ஆழ்வார்

‘‘ओम् नमो नारायणाय’’

|| ஓம் நமோ நாராயணாய ||

"*OM NAMO NARAYANAYA*"

Amalan Adi Piraan, the work of Tiruppaan Alwar has been honored by the renowned Vaishnava Acharyas – Yaamunacharya, his disciples Peria Nambi and Tirumalai Nambi. Acharya Vedantadesika attesting to the spiritual greatness of Alwar's work, wrote a commentary of this work called Munivahana Bhogam in Mani-Pravala style (in Sanskritized Tamil).

Below is given the original verse and translation of one of Tiruppan Alwar's poems demonstrating his profound devotion.

‘Kondal Vannanaik Kovalanaai Vennai
Undavaayan Ennullam Kavarntaanai
Andarkon Ani Arangan Ennamutinaik
Kanda Kankal Matronrinaik Kaanaave”

(Verse 10)

‘I have seen the one whose color is like a dark cloud.
He is Sri Narayana (Sri Ranganatha) who incarnated as Krishna in Gokul and stole the butter collected by the cowherds.
He is the Lord of the celestial beings- Devas.
He is Sri Ranganatha.
He is my nectar (Amrita) and my life.
I had the divine vision of His unparalleled beauty.
What further is there to be seen?!

(“Amalan Adi Piraan”- Poem 10).

Eight

Tirumangai Alwar

“Sri Ramanujacharya, the founder of the Visishtadvaita system of philosophy, has said in his Eulogy of Periya Tirumozhi, the great divine literary and devotional treatise attributed to Tirumangai Alwar:

“Mayonai Vaal-valiyaal Mantiram Kol Mangaiyar Kon”

‘The ruler of Tirumangai region, [Tirumangai Alwar] received the teaching of the most sacred hymn “Om Namo Narayanaya” from Lord Narayana Himself with the force/ strength of his sword”(the story behind this is given later in the chapter).

In the course of his pilgrimage Tirumangai Alwar visited 88 divine places and the Holy shrines dedicated to Lord Narayana in those places. Periya Tirumozhi gives an account of Alwar’s soul stirring experiences on his pilgrimages.”

Tirumangai Alwar (Neelan, the name given to him at birth) was the last of the 12 Alwar Saints. He was a scholar, a ruler of territory in the Chola Kingdom, a composer of devotional hymns and an ardent devotee of Lord Narayana. Tirumangai was born in the 8th century AD into the ‘Kallar’ community in Tiruk kuraiyalur in Chola region of Tamilnadu. Plundering and looting were the means of livelihood of the Kallar community.

“ओम् नमो नारायणाय”

|| ஓம் நமோ நாராயணாய ||

"*OM NAMO NARAYANAYA*"

‘‘ओम् नमो नारायणाय’’

॥ ஓம் நமோ நாராயணாய ॥

"*OM NAMO NARAYANAYA*"

Neelan’s father, Aalinaadar was a Commander in the army of the Chola King, a heroic and a powerful personality. And Neelan’s mother was Vallittiru. During his young years Neelan studied Sanskrit and Tamil treatises. He was also trained in warfare, tribal martial arts and the use of different arms in accordance with the profession of his community.

Neelan followed in the footsteps of his father, showing his heroism by defeating many of the king’s enemies. The Chola King was so pleased by his control of the army, heroic comportment and administrative capacity, that he appointed him as the Ruler of Tiruvali region with Tirumangai as its capital, made him one of his commanders, and honored him with the title of Parakaalan (frightful for enemies). Parakaalan also means “a person beyond time”. He was well-known as Tirumangai Ruler. When he became an ardent devotee of Lord Narayana, and the author of devotional hymns, he became ‘Tirumangai Alwar’. Other names, such as Kaliyan (Man of strength), Kalikanri (destroyer of falsehood) and Kuraiyalur Ruler attached to him as well.

In time Neelan met a beautiful and scholarly Vaishnava girl Kumudavalli. Her foster father was a Vaidya (medical practitioner) in the Tirumangai region. Neelan fell in love with Kumudavalli and with the intention of marrying her, approached her parents with the proposal. Although Neelan had the status of a Ruler, Kumudavalli stipulated two conditions to marry him. The first condition was that Neelan should become a Vaishnava Brahmin and meticulously follow the Vaishnava life style. Because of his deep love for Kumudavalli, Tirumangai ruler accepted this condition. Following the Vaishnava tradition, he wore Vaishnava symbols- conch and disc on his shoulders- and followed the lifestyle and principles of a Vaishnava.

The second condition for marrying Kumudavalli was that Neelan/Tirumangai Ruler should serve and feed 1008 Vaishnava Bhaktas (devotees) every day for a period of one year. He agreed to this condition as well.

Tirumangai Ruler married Kumudavalli, and made elaborate arrangements for the daily feeding of 1008 Vaishnava Bhaktas. This resulted in exhausting all of his wealth. He took recourse in State revenues to pay for the expenses of feeding the Bhaktas daily, as he had promised to his wife. As a subordinate ruler, Tirumangai Ruler was obliged to pay revenues to the Chola King. As a result of depleting of the state revenues, he defaulted on the payment. The King was angered and used his army to extract the payment of dues. The King could not conquer him. In deference to the goodwill that had existed between them, Neelan allowed himself to be imprisoned until payment could be made. But he could not find a way to collect the required funds. He prayed to Lord Narayana to show him the righteous way to pay back the dues, and took a vow not to eat until the King's dues were repaid.

Lord Narayana appeared in Tirumangai Ruler's dream telling him about a treasure hidden on the bank of Vegavati River in Kanchipuram. He asked him to collect that treasure and use it to repay the dues. Tirumangai Ruler followed the Lord's instructions, collected the treasure, and paid the dues to the King. The King was so surprised and pleased by the miracle that he released Tirumangai Ruler, returned the funds to him, and allowed him to use them for the noble cause of feeding the Vaishnava devotees. The funds given by the King, were not sufficient and quickly depleted.

Since Neelan/Tirumangai Ruler did not have sufficient funds to fulfill the second condition stipulated by his wife Kumudavalli, he could find no other source but to resort to Kallar Community's profession of waylaying and robbing rich travelers on the highways.

''ओम् नमो नारायणाय''

॥ ஓம் நமோ நாராயணாய ॥

"*OM NAMO NARAYANAYA*"

''ओम् नमो नारायणाय''

॥ ஓம் நமோ நாராயணாய ॥

"*OM NAMO NARAYANAYA*"

Tirumangai Ruler continued this sinful act of looting the travelers with the aim of continuing to fulfill his wife's condition to serve Lord Narayana's Bhaktas every day. Lord Narayana, with compassion, wished to change this practice of His Bhakta Neelan/Tirumangai Ruler. Despite its being for pious purposes he wanted to end Neelan's sinful practice of robbery.

It is said that Lord Narayana is more pleased by service rendered to Bhaktas than service rendered to Himself. The Lord took the form of a wealthy bridegroom and accompanied by His bride, came in procession through the forest with the wedding party. When Neelan came to know of the approach of the wedding party, he organized his group, surrounded the wedding party and threatened them to part with their jewelry, ornaments and all valuables which they were wearing and carrying.

The wedding party without any resistance acceded to the looter's instruction. Neelan made a bundle of all the jewelry and ornaments. There was one very attractive ring on one of the Bridegroom's toes. When Neelan asked the Bridegroom to remove the ring, The bridegroom said, "he could not remove it" and He wanted Neelan to remove the ring himself. Neelan knelt down, but could not remove the ring. He stretched himself on the ground and successfully removed the ring with his teeth. In this way, he prostrated himself before Lord Narayana and touched the Lord's feet. This sign of Neelan's humility made it possible to remove the ring. When he wanted to leave the place with the bundle of jewelry, ornaments and other valuables, Neelan and his warriors could not lift the bundle. It was too heavy and anchored to the ground.

Neelan became very angry and thought that the bridegroom was a magician, who must be having a 'mantra' with the help of which the bundle could be lifted. He threatened the Bridegroom (Lord) to disclose that mantra. The Lord- in– disguise as the bridegroom, drew Neelan very close to Him and whispered into his ear the most sacred "Ashtakshara (Eight Syllabled) Mantra."

"Om Namo Narayanaya!"

On hearing this most powerful mantra, Neelan/Tirumangai Ruler was greatly influenced, ecstatic tears flowed from his eyes and, he beheld a divine vision of Lord Narayana holding Conch and Disc, with His consort Sridevi/Lakshmi Devi, carried by Garuda.

Spontaneously and with great emotion, he burst into ten beautiful verses and slowly the bridegroom (Lord), bride (Sridevi) and the whole wedding party disappeared. (two of these verses are given below). They appear at the beginning of his grand devotional poetic work "Periya Tirumozhi "(Grand Hymn).

"Taking birth in this world of miseries,
I experienced grief for many years,
foolishly, I tried to find relief in the company of women.
At last my eyes were opened to a world of bliss,
I found the power of the holy name Narayana".

Verse 1

"The holy name of Narayana is the harbinger of all great things,
Such as power, noble family, and wealth,
and eliminates sorrows of the devotee,
It bestows heaven and land.
It blesses with strength and all kinds of good things.
It gives support to the devotee more than even a mother does to a child.
I found all good things by chanting the sacred name Narayana."

Verse 9

‘‘ओम् नमो नारायणाय’’

|| ஓம் நமோ நாராயணாய ||

"OM NAMO NARAYANAYA"

‘‘ओम् नमो नारायणाय’’

॥ ஓம் நமோ நாராயணாய ॥

"*OM NAMO NARAYANAYA*"

By continuously serving the Vaishnava Bhaktas, Tirumangai Ruler became a great devotee of Lord Narayana and went on chanting the sacred Eight-syllabled mantra- [Ashtakshara Mantra] Om! Namo Narayanaya! taught to him by Lord Narayana Himself. Then he completely transformed himself, becoming a devout Vaishnava and giving up the life of the ruler. With a view to atoning for his sins, he continued to praise the qualities, grace and compassion of Lord Narayana and His different incarnations. He visited 88 Holy Vaishnava shrines in different regions of India–both in the south and the north – and wrote beautiful devotional verses in praise of the attributes of the presiding deities of those shrines.

Tirumangai Alwar's Literary and Divine Works

The following six divine works with devotional hymns imbued with Narayana Bhakti and Saranagati Bhava (Devotion and Self Surrender to Lord Narayana) are attributed to Tirumangai Alwar. They constitute almost a third of the Naalaayira Divya Prabandham.

1. The very first grand lyrical devotional work of Tirumangai Alwar is 'Periya Tirumozhi' which comprises 1084 verses presenting the life-story of Alwar. The work starts with Alwar's repentance for indulging in the worldly life of desires and attachments. After receiving the Narayana Mantra from the Lord Himself, he could discriminate between pious and evil aspects of life. Desirous of having a divine vision of Lord Narayana and His Various Incarnations, he undertook a divine pilgrimage of those places where the Lord is present for the benefit of His devotees.

He started his divine journey from the north–the holy Tirup Piriti, also known as Nanda Prayag and continued on to Badrikashram, Shaligram in Nepal, Manasarovar, Naimisharanya, Ahobilam, etc. From there Alwar journied towards the south, going first to Sri Venkata Hill, where he offered his prayers to the Lord Sripati Venkteswara. He continued his pilgrimage to the Vaishnava shrines in Tondai and Chola regions – Tiruvallur, Tiruvallikkeni, Tiruneermalai, Tirukkadal Mallai (Mahabalipuram) Tirukkudantai (Kumbhakonam), Kanchipuram Region and different pilgrimage centers in that Region. His pilgrimage continued to other holy centers including: Tirukkovaloor, Tiruvali, Tirunaraiyur, Tiruchcherai, Terazhuntur, Darbhasayanam, Tirumaliruncholai, Tirukkottiyur, Tirumayyam, Tiruppullani, Tirumokoor, Tirukkurunkudi, etc.

Alwar's descriptions of all the Vaishnava shrines he visited and his ecstatic experiences of devotion to Lord Narayana (the presiding deity in those shrines) as well as the Lord's numerous attributes, are presented with the most sacred lyrical beauty demonstrating Alwar's sense of deep devotion.

Finally, Alwar reached Srirangam, the most sacred City, and remained there in service to the presiding deity Lord Sri Ranganatha. During his time there, with the help he received from the then Pallava Emperor Nandivarman II, he undertook the renovation of the holiest Srirangam temple, the construction of walls and towers and creation of facilities in and around the temple for devotees. He is also credited with introducing the regular recital of Tiruvaimozhi at the Srirangam Temple being a great admirer of Nammalwar the author of Tiruvaimozhi.

''ओम् नमो नारायणाय''

|| ஓம் நமோ நாராயணாய ||

"*OM NAMO NARAYANAYA*"

‘‘ओम् नमो नारायणाय’’

॥ ஓம் நமோ நாராயணாய ॥

"*OM NAMO NARAYANAYA*"

In summary, Tirumangai Alwar's Periya Tirumozhi can be called "An Anthology of Divine and Sacred Vaishnava Shrines" offering a description of Alwar's extensive holy pilgrimage covering 88 sacred places.

2 through 6:

The 5 other shorter works attributed to Tirumangai Alwar are as follows:

Tirukkuruntandakam, Tiruneduntandakam, Tiruvezhu Kootrirukkai, Siriya Tirumadal, and Periya Tirumadal.

2. **Tirukkuruntandakam :** This work consists of 20 verses of four lines each, composed in the Tamil meter Tandakam. The verses describe the devotee's deep love for Lord Narayana. The Devotee and the Lord are likened to Nayika and Nayaka – consort and beloved separated from the former. Alwar, the devotee is extremely pleased to have Narayana in his heart, and decides to never allow the Lord to separate from him; He would hold on to Him like a baby monkey clinging to its mother.

   Alwar also sings the praises of the sacred Vaishnava places - Tirumaliruncholai, Tirukkudantai, Srirangam, Tirupati and Tirupper and details the attributes of the presiding deity - Lord Narayana- in those places.

3. **Tiruneduntandakam :** As the title suggests, the verses in this treatise have also been composed in Tandakam meter. This is larger than the previous treatise, as indicated by the words used in the title 'Kuru' and 'Nedu', meaning small and big respectively. Tiruneduntandakam consists of 30 verses in which Alwar has praised Lord Narayana as well as described his devotion to the Lord and his desire for an

ecstatic devotional experience. Alwar also chronicles the qualities and divine deeds of Lord Narayana's Incarnations- Vamana, Rama, Krishna and Parasurama, describes the sacred places Tirukkovaloor, Tiruvoorakam, Tiruneerakam, Tirupper, and Tiruvehka and the greatness of the presiding deities of those shrines.

Here too Alwar becomes Nayika (consort) separated from her Nayaka (beloved) and describes her pangs of separation and all-consuming desire to be with her beloved Narayana.

4. **Tiruvezhukootrirukkai :** This small treatise provides the definition of the following five forms of the Lord Narayana's existence and expounds on the quality of His being Parabrahma (Supreme Being). It describes Alwar's Self-Surrender at the sacred feet of Lord Narayana, (specifically dwelling at the holy place of Kumbhakonam, where the presiding deity Narayana supine on Adisesha) praying to be released from the obstacles along the path to attain the Lord. This prayer of Tirumangai Alwar is similar to the prayer by Nammalwar* to whom Tirumangai is completely dedicated.

   - Para, Lord Narayana remaining in Vaikunta, His transcendental abode.
   - Vyuha, Lord Vishnu in Yoga-Nidra (Yogic slumber) on Adisesha on the milky ocean.
   - Antaryami. All-pervading Lord Narayana dwelling in the hearts of His creations in the universe.
   - Vibhava, Lord Narayana coming to the earth in different incarnations (Avatars) to protect Dharma.

''ओम् नमो नारायणाय''

|| ஓம் நமோ நாராயணாய ||

"OM NAMO NARAYANAYA"

* this prayer can be seen in Tiruvaimozhi, Section 5, sub-section 8, Verse 7.

‘‘ओम् नमो नारायणाय’’

॥ ஓம் நமோ நாராயணாய ॥

"OM NAMO NARAYANAYA"

- Archa, Lord Narayana in Image Incarnations/ Manifestations as Idols or Sacred Symbols for the purpose of being worshipped in the Temples and at homes.

Sri Ramanuja, the founder of the Visishtadwaita school of Indian Philosophy, acknowledged the greatness of Tirumangai Alwar in his two verses at the beginning of this treatise:

"By meditating on this work, the whole universe could escape from its miseries."

5. **Siriya Tirumadal :** It is a shorter, but masterly sentimental poem. It celebrates the Bhakta's love for Lord Narayana, while at the same time, expressing his distress at being apart from the Lord.

The devotee (bhakta) Alwar in his singular desire to become one with Lord Narayana (Nayaka; the beloved), becomes Nayika (loving maiden) and expresses her deep sense of anguish at being separated from her Beloved (Narayana). As such it is a literary composition of loving devotion, a love poem filled with Nayika's despair at separation. Seeing Nayika's restless and agitated state, her mother consulted a fortune teller who informs her that her daughter (Nayika) is distressed due to the acts of the Supreme. It is He who is responsible.

To relieve herself of her misery Nayika (Devotee Alwar) announces her decision to perform an observance** - (consisting of fasting and riding on a horse made of palm leaves) around the sacred places where the Lord Supreme is present in archavatara (different divine image incarnations). This latter rite is performed by Nayika to make her deep love for the Nayaka known to the public and gain the public sympathy and elicit support in helping her reunite with her Nayaka.

** This Observance is called Madal Vrata in Tamil, often depicted in the ancient Tamil literary tradition.

Acharya Sri Ramanuja

"ओम् नमो नारायणाय"

॥ ஓம் நமோ நாராயணாய ॥

"*OM NAMO NARAYANAYA*"

‘‘ओम् नमो नारायणाय’’

॥ ஓம் நமோ நாராயணாய ॥

"OM NAMO NARAYANAYA"

6. **Periya Tirumadal :** Siriya Tirumadal and Periya Tirumadal, both contain almost the same content, but differ in size; the former is short and brief and the latter large and extensive. The titles themselves indicate this difference; Periya is Large & Siriya is Short. Both are love poems filled with the devotee Alwar's Viraha- Bhakti- subtle expression of the pain of separation from the beloved Lord Narayana.

   Tirumangai Alwar was dedicated to Nammalwar. As described earlier in Chapter 5, Nammalwar's four treatises are recognized as the essence of the four Vedas – Tiru Viruttam, Tiruvaasiriyam, Periya Tiruvantadi and Tiruvaimozhi as the essence of Rigveda, Yajurveda, Atharva Veda and Saama Veda respectively.

   It is a belief among scholars that the six treatises of Tirumangai Alwar are like the Six limbs of the Nammalwar's four Vedas- Siksha, Kalpa, Nirukta, Chanda, Jyotisha and Vyakarana,***

   In summary, Tirumangai Alwar's six literary treatises present the legend of a devotee's slave- like and loving devotion to Lord Narayana with the spiritual discipline of self-surrender or Prapatti.

***
Siksha- The science which teaches proper pronunciation of words
Kalpa- The science which lays down the rituals and prescribes the rules for sacrificial and ceremonial Acts
Nirukta- Etymological interpretation
Chanda- Metrical science; prosody
Jyotisha- Astronomical science
Vyakarana - Grammatical analysis

TIRUVARANGATTU AMUTHANAR
திருவரங்கத்து அமுதனார்

அமுதனாருடைய குருபக்தியும் நாராயண பக்தியும் நிறைந்த அந்தாதியின் சுருக்கம் கீழே ஆங்கிலத்தில் கொடுக்கப்பட்டுள்ளது.

(இராமானுஜ நூற்றந்தாதி)

A summary of Amuthanar's work filled with devotion to his Preceptor and Lord Narayana is given below in English.

(Iramanuja Nootrantadi)

"In every verse of Amuthanar's work Iramanuja Nootrantadi, we find his deep devotion to his Guru Sri Ramanujacharya; Amuthanar in each poem sings the Guru's name, Guru's divine qualities and the essence of Guru Bhakti."

“ओम् नमो नारायणाय”

॥ ஓம் நமோ நாராயணாய ॥

"*OM NAMO NARAYANAYA*"

Vaishnava Saint & Acharya Sri Ramanuja's disciple Tiruvarangattu Amuthanar

Vaishnava Saint Tiruvarangattu Amuthanar, the author of "Iramanuja Nootrantadi" was born in the holy City of Srirangam in Tiruchchinapalli District in Tamilnadu in a family of Moongil Kudi. His name (Tiruvarangattu- related to Srirangam) indicates that he was born in Srirangam.

After studying vedas and the religious scriptures, he worked as a priest attending to the temple activities and offering discourses on Puranas in the Srirangam Temple. For this reason, he became known as Periya Kovil Nambi (Servant of big Temple -Srirangam Temple)

Tiruvarangattu Amuthanar was a contemporary of Sri Ramanujacharya (1017 AD - 1137 AD), the founder of the Visishtadvaita (Qualified non-dualism) system of Indian philosophy. Initially Amuthanar was an Advaitee, a follower of the philosophy of non-dualism promoted by Adi Sankaracharya.

Later, having been influenced by the Saint Kooraththazhvan, the disciple of Sri Ramanuja, he became the devotee and follower of Sri Ramanuja. In devotion to Sri Ramanuja, he wrote 108 poems honoring and praising Sri Ramanuja. Collectively these poems are known as Iramanuja Nootrantadi and constitute the concluding part of "Naalaayira Divya Prabandham".

Amuthanar's Nootrantadi has been recognized as 'Gayatri' for the devotees immersed in self-surrender and devotion to Lord Narayana and is known as "Prapanna Gayatri" and "Prapanna Savitri" (Gayatri or Savitri is considered sacred treatise for the Lord's devotees and for those who have fully surrendered to Lord Narayana).

In every poem of Amuthanar's work we find his deep devotion (Guru Bhakti) to his Guru Sri Ramanujacharya. Amuthanar sings the Guru's name and praises his greatness in each of the 108 poems signifying its spiritual quality.

Whereas Alwars' works are the descriptive, devotional and philosophic treatises pertaining to Narayana Bhakti, Tiruvarangattu Amuthanar's songs describe the essence of Guru-Bhakti and the divine qualities of Guru Sri Ramanujacharya. We find the same description of Guru - Bhakti in the divine hymns of Madurakavi Alwar who extolls his preceptor Nammalwar (Shatagopa).

The title 'Iramanuja Nootrantadi' means 100 Antadi verses which praise Guru Sri Ramanujacharya. But the book contains 108 verses which are significant as the Vedic hymns, consequently Amuthanar's spiritually imbued Iramanuja Nootrantadi is called 'Prapanna Gayatri' and 'Prapanna Savitri' as stated above.

For the devotees of the Lord Narayana, who have surrendered at His feet with utter humility and faith (Prapatti), Amuthanar's work is recognized as Gayatri/ Vedic treatise.

The most notable qualities of Amuthanar's work- Iramanuja Nootrantadi are as follows:

''ओम् नमो नारायणाय''

|| ஓம் நமோ நாராயணாய ||

"*OM NAMO NARAYANAYA*"

''ओम् नमो नारायणाय''

॥ ஓம் நமோ நாராயணாய ॥

"OM NAMO NARAYANAYA"

Acharya Ramanuja himself, in presence of his disciples-Kooratthazhvan, Andavan, Embar, etc. listened to Amuthanar's work recited in Amuthanar's own voice.

Acharya was extremely pleased to listen to Amuthanar's 'nectar like sweet voice', hence he honored him by naming him as Amuthanar (sweet like nectar). From then he became known as Tiruvarangattu Amuthanar (Amuthanar living in the sacred city Srirangam).

Alwars' Book of these divine verses- Naalayira Divya Prabandham- continues to be recited regularly in the temples and during the festivals. At the end of the Divya Prabandham recital, as per the tradition, only the last two verses of each Prabandham are recited repeatedly whereas in the case of Amuthanar's work, the last 3 verses [verses 106, 107 and 108] are recited. This is considered a great honor.

Amuthanar's work is a unique treatise explaining the greatness of Guru Sri Ramanujacharya and Guru- Bhakti [devotion to Guru]. It is recited as a daily prayer by Vaishnava devotees. The basic premise of this work is that salvation is possible only with the Guru-Kripa (Guru's Grace).

Amuthanar's work describes Sri Ramanuja's reverential praise for all Alwars and his respect for the earlier Acharyas -Nathamuni and Yamunacharya (known in Tamil as Aalavantar) who presented the basis for Visishtadwaita (Philosophy of qualified non-dualism) and whose principles of Vedic Philosophy provided the founding tenets of VIsishtadwaita.

The most important ingredient of VIsishtadwaita is the philosophy of Bhakti and Prapatti, described by Alwars, particularly Nammalwar which can be seen as the authentic source for Ramanuja's philosophic principles. The impact of Alwars' Bhakti philosophy can be seen in the Visishtadwaita doctrine expounded through Ramanujacharya's Works, Sri Bhashya, Gita

Bhashya, etc. These works are replete with Ramanuja's reverence for Alwars and their philosophy.

Sri Ramanuja was a great devotee of Nammalwar whose Tiruvaimozhi- the Tamil Veda- was propagated and popularized by him through his Visishtadwaita Doctrine as described by Amuthanar in some of the verses in his Nootrantadi. (Verses 19, 29, 46, 54)

Amuthanar's devotion to his Guru Sri Ramanuja was so profound that he emphatically asserts that if Sri Ramanuja accepted him as his devotee, he would be indifferent to liberation (Moksha) or hell (Narak). (verse 30).

Amuthanar's treatise further indicates the extent to which the society of that time was influenced by the six non-Vedic sects- i.e. Jains, Buddhists, Ajivikas, Charvakas, Kaanadas and Pasupatas and how Sri Ramanuja defied and defeated them in his discourses, disputations, and through his writings like Gita Bhashya, etc. In so doing he established the greatness and importance of Vedic principles, the path of Bhakti and Prapatti (devotion and surrender) to Lord Narayana, devotion to the Lord's devotees (Daasa bhakti) and their devotees (Daasaanudaasa Bhakti) and popularized the Visishtadwaita school of philosophy expounded by Sri Ramanuja.

(verses 48, 79, 93, 99 etc.)

''ओम् नमो नारायणाय''

|| ஓம் நமோ நாராயணாய ||

"OM NAMO NARAYANAYA"

‘‘ओम् नमो नारायणाय’’

॥ ஓம் நமோ நாராயணாய ॥

"*OM NAMO NARAYANAYA*"

Appendix Two

Conclusion
Alwars and Acharyas

Alwars

In the previous chapters, we studied a brief history of the philosophy of deep devotion and service to Lord Narayana and self-surrender (Bhakti and Prapatti) at the feet of the Supreme Lord- Para Brahma (Narayana) as well as the life and works of the mystical, devotional Vaishnava poets and their meditative, spiritual and ecstatic philosophic thoughts.

These poets -ALWARS- are the sacred advocates of deep meditation and mystical devotion, and devotees of the spiritual attributes of the supreme Lord, Narayana. Alwars' Bhakti verses (devotional poems) collected and compiled by Nathamuni are designated as Divya Prabandham or Naalayira Divya Prabandham [4000 divine verses]. The socially inclusive Vaishnava poetic devotionalism of Alwars has been the basis of the systematically developed Vaishnava Theology popularized by scholastic preceptors who are known as Acharyas.

Acharyas

Tradition of Vaishnava Acharyas

The Tradition of Vaishnava Acharyas begins with the philosopher-poet and the founder of Tamil Vedas, Nammalwar (Shatagopa-9th century). His works are considered Tamil Vedas and are treated as the basis for the Visishtadvaita school of philosophy.

There were Acharyas in every century until the 15th century. Noteworthy among them are:

- Nathamuni (9th century A.D.)

  Nammalwar's disciple, Nathamuni compiled and collected the complete works of all Alwars as desired by his Guru Nammalwar. Nammalwar was the foremost Alwar as well as Acharya and the founder of Tamil Veda (Vedam Tamil seitha Piran).
- Yamunacharya (also Known as Aalavandar, 10th to 11th centuries); Yamunacharya's disciple Periya Nambi, who in turn was the preceptor to Sri Ramanuja.
- Sri Ramanuja (11th to 12th centuries).
- After Sri Ramanuja the Guru-Sishya or Acharya tradition continued with eminent acharyas- Embar; Parasara Bhattar; Pillai Lokacharya; and Manavala Mamuni (15th century A. D.).
- Guru-Sishya or Acharya tradition ended with Manavala Mamuni.

Another brilliant Acharya who belonged to the post-Ramanuja period was Sri Vedanta Desika (13th century).

The followers of Acharya Sri Ramanuja respect the Tamil Vedas (Divya Prabandham) more than the Sanskrit Vedas- (Southern Tradition of Vaishnavism is called TENKALAI in Tamil) whereas those of Acharya Sri Vedanta Desika honor equally the Tamil Vedas (Divya Prabandham) and Sanskrit Vedas- (Northern Tradition of Vaishnavism is called- VADAKALAI in Tamil)

''ओम् नमो नारायणाय''

|| ஓம் நமோ நாராயணாய ||

"OM NAMO NARAYANAYA"

Acharya /Teacher – Disciple Lineage

Teacher	**Disciple**
Nammalwar (9th century A.D.)	Nathamuni
Nathamuni	Uyyankondar
Uyyankondar	Manakkal Nambi
Manakkal Nambi.	Aalavantar (Yamunacharya)
Yamunacharya	Periya Nambi
Periya Nambi.	Ramanuja
Ramanuja.	Embar (12th century A.D.)
Embar	Parasara Bhattar
Parasara Bhattar.	Nanjeeyar
Nanjeeyar.	Nampillai
Nampillai.	Vadakkut Tiruveetippillai
Vadakkut Tiruveetippillai	Pillai Lokacharya
Pillai Lokacharya.	Tiruvaimozhippillai
Tiruvaimozhippillai. (15th century A.D.)	Manavala Mamuni

''ओम् नमो नारायणाय''

॥ ஓம் நமோ நாராயணாய ॥

"OM NAMO NARAYANAYA"